Praise for Big League Life

"Chip Scarinzi has written a beautiful baseball story, full of the highs and lows and day-to-day drama of a season. As the story unfolds, the reader is introduced to the many layers and personalities that form an inside look at life in the big leagues. A most enjoyable read and recommended for any fan of America's pastime." – **Ken Korach**, Oakland Athletics' broadcaster and author of *Holy Toledo*

"With Big League Life, Scarinzi immerses readers in the life of a Major League team, starting in the preseason and continuing all the way to the postseason. As the story of his fictional club unfurls, Scarinzi taps into the hope, frustration, redemption, joy, and heartbreak that the game's most magical seasons evoke. His characters and their team bring to life those qualities that led so many of us to fall in love with the game in the first place." – **Josh Pahigian**, author of *The Ultimate Baseball Road Trip* and *The Amazing Baseball Adventure*

"A delightful journey onto the diamond, through the dugout, and into the lives that shape a Major League ball club. The author wonderfully navigates a team's many personalities and offers a glimpse into the beating heart of today's modern game." – **Scott Butler**, author of *So You Think You're a Philadelphia Phillies Fan?*

Big League Life

A NOVEL

CHIP SCARINZI

Rowe Publishing

ISBN 13: 978-1-64446-013-9

1 3 5 7 9 8 6 4 2

Printed in the United States of America
Published by

R
Rowe Publishing
www.rowepub.com

For my mother, Dana.

The Players

JOHN MCGOWN. Retired journeyman infielder and current manager of the Philadelphia Phillies.

MARK JOHNSON. General Manager for the Phillies and one of the more promising front office executives in the game.

BENNETT PETERSON. Left-handed relief pitcher who comes to the Phillies' Spring Training camp hoping to resuscitate a flagging career.

MARCEL VALENTÍN. Utility infielder better known for his leadership skills and defensive talent than for his hitting ability.

MIKE BRASHEAR. Nicknamed "Brash," the young second baseman has emerged as one of the top minor league prospects in the game.

AARON TANNER. A starting pitcher with superstar potential. The "Ace" of the Phillies starting rotation.

PEDRO ARROYO. The Phillies' gruff pitching coach pulls no punches and his staff loves him for it.

JESSICA TANNER. Wife to Aaron Tanner, Jessica serves as the glue that keeps the family together during the long and winding baseball season.

PAUL SMITH. A left-handed relief pitcher that has served as a steady presence in big league bullpens for many years.

ABIGAIL PETERSON. Wife to Bennett Peterson and the steady presence for the big reliever in a baseball life that has been anything but steady.

MARCUS COOPER. Head scout for the Phillies.

FINN BRESLIN. Scout for the Minnesota Twins.

BARRETT TAYLOR. The Phillies' gregarious first baseman.

RAUL VALENCIA. Former catcher making the transition to Phillies third baseman. Valencia and Taylor serve as significant sources of power in the Phillies batting lineup.

ALEX CORINO. Head of baseball research and analytics for the Phillies.

HANNAH CHANNING. Talented Phillies scout who reports to Marcus Cooper.

TOM FLANAGAN. *Philadelphia Inquirer* sports reporter on the Phillies beat.

REBECCA STOYANOS. Phillies beat writer for PhillyVoice.com, one of several online-only media outlets that burst onto the scene in recent years.

MARK DORFMAN. A mainstay in the Phillies press box, covering the team on behalf of a Delaware County-based daily newspaper.

GREGORY WILCOX. Third baseman at Vanderbilt and one of several ballplayers the Phillies scout ahead of the annual Amateur Draft.

DANIEL BAKER. Veteran starting pitcher for the Phillies in the twilight of his career.

PATRICK SHERIDAN. Team doctor for the Phillies.

RICHIE LEGRANDE. Outfielder for the Phillies who struggles with balancing his life on and off the field.

PRESTON SAUNDERS. Superstar in the making, Saunders patrols center field for the Phillies and serves as a crucial part of the team's core of talented, young ballplayers.

TYSON JACKSON. Outfielder who joins the Phillies midseason after being traded.

RUBEN ALMORA. Mark Jackson's counterpart in Houston, Almora serves as General Manager for the Astros.

ROD CLEARY. Bench coach for the Lehigh Valley IronPigs, Triple-A affiliate of the Phillies.

LEONARD PRIES. Longtime play-by-play broadcaster for the Phillies, Pries serves as "the voice of summer" for baseball fans across the region.

HENRY LORENZO. Color commentator who brings anecdotes and analysis to the action that unfolds on the field.

JOSE ALVAREZ. Promising rookie shortstop for the Phillies.

JUAN HERNANDEZ. Third base coach for the Phillies.

RYAN DOLAN. A jack of all trades, he splits his time in the field with Valentín as a platoon second baseman.

MARCUS BERGMAN. Plays for the Lehigh Valley IronPigs and hopes to catch the eye of the big league ballclub.

VICTOR CRUZ. Manager of the Lehigh Valley IronPigs.

SETH ROSENTHAL. Agent for Bennett Peterson.

RICK TOPERICK. Veteran catcher for the Phillies appreciated for his ability to navigate pitchers through a ballgame.

JAVIER ALVAREZ. Veteran of Cuba's Baseball Federation and brother to Jose Alvarez.

Contents

1 – The Manager 1

2 – The Veteran 10

3 – The Ace 16

4 – Tough Decisions 21

5 – Road to Redemption 29

6 – Life On the Road 35

7 – Struggles 41

8 – Quiet Moments 47

9 – Draft Preparations 54

10 – On the Beat 62

11 – Draft Day 70

12 – UCL 79

13 – Trade Winds Blowing 84

14 – Change of Scenery 91

15 – A Star Arrives 96

16 – The GM 103

17 – The Prospect 109

18 – The Sound of Summer 115

19 – Star-Crossed 122

20 – Abigail 129

21 – Standing Pat 134

CONTENTS

22 – A Strange New World 140

23 – Crunching Numbers 146

24 – A Bump In the Road 152

25 – Fight Club 157

26 – September 1 165

27 – Three and Twenty-One 170

28 – The Story 176

29 – #162 .181

30 – Baseball's Second Season 189

31 – The Best of Times 195

32 – The Aftermath 200

33 – The End Is a Beginning 207

34 – Postscript to a Championship 214

Acknowledgments 223

About the Author 227

Other Books by the Author 229

1
The Manager

Dew-tipped grass glistened in the early morning sunlight along Florida's Gulf Coast. For John McGown, however, it may as well have been the middle of the night as he toiled at his desk beneath the hum of antiseptic fluorescent lights. Somewhere beyond his office door, a narrow concrete corridor led to practice fields where 62 grown men stretched, ran drills, and played catch like schoolboys on the sandlot. This wasn't the big leagues – not yet, at least – but it was as close as it gets in late February.

Not long ago, the man known to many as "Mac" was one of those young upstarts basking in the sun, preparing for a new baseball season with wide-eyed optimism. In parts of nine seasons with the Chicago Cubs, Milwaukee Brewers, San Diego Padres, and Houston Astros, he squeezed enough out of middling athletic abilities to survive the final cuts of Spring Training on a couple of occasions. Other times, he shuttled back and forth between the majors and minors for a few games here and there, filling in when bona fide big leaguers hit the shelf or found themselves on the outbound end of a trade. In 1992, he amassed 346 plate appearances and batted an adequate .275 with some pop at the plate and above-average speed on the base paths. That season, the high-water mark in an under-the-radar pro career, remains tucked away among his most cherished memories of life in The Show.

Now, many years later, McGown was a leader of men and the manager of the Philadelphia Phillies. Alongside the team's General Manager, he'd spend the next month studying the performance of those 62 men plying their craft on practice fields in Clearwater, Florida, and hope to land on the right mix of talent to fill 26 roster spots before heading north.

"What's the good word, John?" An upbeat voice called from the doorway, bringing McGown out of his studies. The sound echoed off cement walls, painted to appear less like a prison cell, but still lacking the comforts of home.

"Hey, Mark. You know how it is." Mark Johnson, the young GM with an economics degree from Princeton, joined McGown at his desk, still tidy in these early days of Spring Training. As the weeks progressed, however, paperwork and half-empty takeout coffee cups would decorate every inch of the wooden desktop. There was a method to his madness, he would say. He had built enough trust with the front office in his six years on the job that they let him do as he pleased – mostly. "Just learning about my guys. I like this shortstop you found. Alvarez. The Cuban kid. He looks like a player."

"I hope so. It's a crapshoot sometimes."

"Juan will work with him." McGown tossed his paperwork aside and leaned back, staring just above Johnson's head at a panoramic photo of the team's stadium up north. "He can move, he's fluid. Good hands; looks like a good gloveman and I think the bat will translate."

"That's kind of what our guy saw down there. If he can make the adjustment, he could hit 30 bombs, win a Gold Glove, and make me look like a genius." It's easy to predict greatness in February, but plucking Jose Alvarez from Cuban ball in late December was touted by many optimists as Johnson's master stroke of the offseason. Johnson ascended to his position after several years of tutelage under his much-loved predecessor Charlie Joyce. Joyce, entering his mid-70s, had stepped down to make way for the up-and-coming Johnson whom the respected baseball man had groomed to take over when the time came. Still connected to the team as a special advisor, Joyce sang Johnson's praises to anyone who would listen and, in the years since, most would agree that the transition had been a smooth one. Even-keeled and fair, Johnson carried himself with the professionalism and polish of a man with far more experience and advanced age. At 38, he was among the league's youngest and least experienced general managers. An argument could also be made, however, that a series of shrewd roster moves and his efforts to revamp the team's scouting operations put Johnson in the conversation among the league's most promising executives.

"We'll get him there. He's a special kind of athlete. Juan can bring out the best in him." Juan was Juan Fernandez, third base coach for the Phillies and a man who gained passage from Cuba the hard way many years earlier before a near Hall of Fame career in the Phillies infield. If anyone could tap into Alvarez' immense potential, it was Fernandez.

"You like the rest of the squad?" Johnson grabbed a bottle of water from a case resting against the wall and took a long sip.

"I do."

"Think we've got 26 big leaguers in camp?"

"I do."

"I think we'll really surprise some people this season," Johnson gave McGown a gentle pat on the shoulder. The two men had taken different paths to their assigned posts, but despite their generational and philosophical differences, both men enjoyed the company and perspective of the other. "You'll get 'em ready and then we'll go out there and win our fair share of ballgames."

"We just might, Mark. Think we're building a winner." As his GM departed, McGown turned his attention to another sheet of paper with those same 62 names listed in the right-hand column and an empty lineup card along the left. Not everyone would make the team or the expanded 40-man roster, of course. Many of the athletes that cluttered the practice fields and locker room had no illusions that their destiny rested with the big league club – or even anywhere within the organization. At this early stage of the season, when Opening Day is still beyond the horizon, everyone gets a chance to play. It's like the sandlot all over again, only with 62 men vying for an opportunity, a chance to be noticed. Some more desperate than others, some "just getting their work in," as the saying goes. McGown leaned in closer and began to write out the first lineup card for the first exhibition game of a brand-new season. Like a chemist, he would spend the next several weeks mixing and matching components, blending abilities together in search of that perfect lineup card – the winning combination he hoped to use for the better part of 162 regular season games. As the weeks pass, the roster would thin out and the locker room, a sea of humanity today, would retract to more manageable numbers. He only hoped that talent would reveal itself before decision time. Truth be told, every manager lives in fear of the one that got away, the can't-miss star who thrives in another organization. McGown exhaled as his pen touched the paper.

Saunders, CF.

McGown knew who would be leading off for the ball club on Opening Day barring injury and, as custom dictated, he made certain to pencil that man into his first lineup of the spring slate. Preston Saunders was a success story if there ever was one. A local kid, he grew up in South Philly and never left. Embarking on his fourth campaign with the team of his childhood dreams, he grabbed ahold of a starting centerfield opening as a rookie and, three All-Star appearances and one batting title later, never looked back. A true five-tool player, equal parts bat, glove, and speed, Saunders promised to be a fixture for the Phillies for many years to come.

Valentín, 2B.

Marcel Valentín had little chance of making the team out of Spring Training and at this stage of his career, he was at peace with those long odds. At 34 years of age, he entered camp hoping to showcase the grit and hustle that made him a frequent resident of Spring Training rosters each year. This season represented his eleventh non-roster invitation to big league camp and by the end of March, he could always count on a handshake, and a fresh assignment in someone's minors league system. Such is the life of the non-roster invitee. While a guaranteed roster spot would be a dream come true, Valentín understood his role and he was comfortable with it. A well above-average second baseman, Valentín carried a reputation around the league as a coach on the field. He worked with prospects, exhibited model behavior, and always stepped up as best he could when opportunity came calling. Bringing a .239 lifetime batting average and only 832 plate appearances into his fourteenth professional season, Valentín's future in the big leagues rested between his ears: it was a commonly held belief that Valentín would make an excellent manager upon the occasion of his retirement. In the meantime, McGown penciled him into the second spot in his lineup as a reward to a guy who reminded him quite a bit of himself.

Alvarez, SS.

McGown smiled as he penciled the youngster into the most important position on the field and in the lineup. *No sense holding back*, he thought. As the manager saw it, there was a great deal of benefit to tossing him into the fire and seeing how he responds.

"Mac, can I have a moment?" McGown looked up from his work to find a husky, bearded man in the doorway. Bennett Peterson, a journeyman reliever, had an outside shot at breaking camp with the big club on account of his left arm. It's no secret across Major League Baseball that if you throw from the left side and have a pulse, you have a decent shot at finding work. Left-handed relievers capable of lighting up the radar gun like Peterson, however, were an even more coveted breed. Electric when able to locate his fastball and a devastating slider, the matter of location had caused enough headaches throughout an under-whelming career to limit his ability to hang onto a roster spot. Now on the wrong side of 30, Peterson had begun to recognize that perceptions about his abilities were already formed. He was running out of chances to prove that he could stick. McGown pushed his chemistry project aside and waved the big reliever forward.

"Come on in, take a seat." McGown removed his glasses and gave the mountain of a man seated across his desk a once-over. He could feel the young man's nerves boiling beneath the surface. All players grapple with their own mortality at some point in their career and it appeared that Peterson's time had arrived. "What's on your mind, Ben?"

"I just want you to know that I feel real good; I had a great offseason and, I don't know, it just clicked for me." Sweat beaded along Peterson's brow and the chair creaked as he shifted his weight in constant movement. "I think this is going to be a big year for me. I've put in a lot of work and I know I can help this team."

McGown smiled. He was 32 when he had this same conversation with another manager in another stale, cement Spring Training office. At that time, more years in the past than he cared to remember, he felt the end coming and while his body had slowed, his brain wasn't ready to give it up. Peterson was battling those same thoughts a few years earlier, it seemed.

"Ben, how many years have you been in the league?"

"Five years, Mac. I've got a lot left in the tank. A lot of mileage left in my left arm." He patted his shoulder for effect. True enough, Peterson had steered well clear of the disabled list during his short career. Plus, he had never logged more than 30 big league innings in any of his five seasons on account of his erratic performance.

"I tend to agree with that sentiment." McGown pulled a baseball card off a pin-marked bulletin board above his desk. "Do you know this man?"

"Charlie Sutter. A real old-timer; spent a long time in the game." Peterson flipped the card around in his over-sized hands and studied the statistics on the back. "Good numbers."

"Good player, even better manager." McGown appreciated the way his pitcher studied the card. That attention to detail was a sign of a player who wanted to learn – a student of the game and a man who could be coached. "I was in your shoes once and he told me, 'the end comes for all of us. It's not your time.'"

"Yeah?" Peterson looked up from the trading card, though his anxiety kept him from making eye contact with his manager.

"That's right." McGown leaned forward. "Son, it's not your time. I think you can help us this season. Just keep it simple – calm your nerves and let it fly."

Peterson couldn't hide his relief as both men stood and shook hands. Pulling the bill of his hat low across his brow, he gave the older man a nod and made a tight turn around the door frame. The sound of cleats rattling across the cement corridor echoed until he escaped back into the late-morning sunshine and the salty breeze of Florida's Gulf Coast. McGown turned his attention back to his own study, messing with paperwork to remind himself of what he had been doing before the interruption. Alvarez. Of course, the talent-rich wild card, currently penciled into the premier hitting slot in the team's lineup. Equal parts expectation and reflection of how highly he's regarded within the organization. *Best if he understands from the start how we view him*, McGown thought.

Toperick, C.

One benefit of the Spring Training exhibit slate is that it gave McGown a chance to drop players into unconventional positions in the lineup that he would never consider when the results mattered. To that end, Rick Toperick, primed to bat cleanup in McGown's first lineup of the spring, was breaking new ground with his promotion up the lineup. A fixture in the eight-hole for years, Toperick was never a middle-of-the-lineup producer and, importantly, had never been asked to be that kind of player. Rather, his managers had long been forced to find a way to keep him in the lineup because of his defense behind the plate. For as suspect as his batting performance had been through the years, his ability to call a game and carry young pitchers through pressure-cooker, high-leverage situations was so good it overshadowed his faults. Toperick was an asset for a young pitching staff finding its way. Of course, he was also sharp enough to know he wasn't batting clean-up due to newfound confidence in his hitting ability. The Phillies had a power-hitting catching prospect working his way through the minors and, as is customary in Spring Training, Toperick would grab a couple at-bats before giving way to the youngster.

Toperick's mission during the early spring months, much like Valentín though with the comfort of a secured spot on the roster, was to pass on as much knowledge as he could to the Phillies' presumptive catcher of the future. He would dutifully keep the position warm until sometime down the road when the organization determined that the young understudy was ready to take the next step. Would that time come this season? At this stage, it was impossible to know.

McGown looked at his watch and pushed the page aside. The rest of the batting order would have to wait. There would be plenty of time to concoct the perfect lineup. For now, it was high time he stepped out of the dungeon and into the light.

In a league obsessed with data and number-crunching, McGown still enjoyed watching ballplayers play ball. He embraced the shift toward analytics and loved the Phillies' infusion of smart, talented data scientists into a Front Office that for too long had been beset by antiquated thinking. Still, he always found that there's something about the fluidity of a player's movement and his natural ability that hadn't fully translated into numbers – not yet, at least. *You can't have one without the other*, he thought. A manager can learn a great deal just by watching a player move around the diamond. Analysis aside, even after a half-century McGown still loved watching baseball. On this day, while 62 players of varying abilities and potential played catch and ran drills, he imagined he always would.

2

The Veteran

"Ándale! Ándale! Move, move, move!"

A diminutive man stood atop the first base bag, shouting orders while watching his much younger teammate scamper across the dirt infield as if his feet were on fire. The man racing toward a bouncing white ball, woven strips of cowhide and yarn, would not get there in time. Despite a headlong dive, Mike Brashear, a promising middle infield prospect, watched the ball sneak between the second base bag and his outstretched glove, slowing as it reached the thick outfield grass. Drenched with sweat, uniform caked in dirt, Brashear rested on his stomach to catch his breath.

"Did you see what happened there?" Marcel Valentín hopped off the first base bag and jogged over to his prone teammate.

"I hesitated."

"You hesitated. You *cannot* hesitate." With an outstretched arm, he pulled the younger man to his feet, dusted off his jersey, and pointed toward the cage enveloping the batter's box where the team's bench coach rested, bat in hand, waiting for the fielding tutorial to conclude before taking his next swing. "You've got a righty in the box. You have an idea of where that ball is headed. Trust your instincts, move with the crack of the bat."

"I'll get to it next time – I can feel it coming. It's starting to feel more natural." The two men had been on the infield dirt performing for an audience of teammates for just over an hour.

"Good. That's the idea – we're gonna get you a Gold Glove yet!" Valentín laughed and returned to his perch on first base. "Okay, vamos. Let's go again."

If the Phillies' front office needed more reason to keep the veteran utility man around, his after-hours work with the team's top prospects served as Exhibit A. Closing in on mid-March, an argument could be made that his Spring Training performance was Exhibit B. Stricken with the "all-glove, no-bat" curse at the onset of his career, Valentín was having the best spring of his life. Playing at least a few innings every day, one benefit of the exhibition slate and its split-squad games, he found his hitting stroke early and never let up. Showing excellent gap-to-gap power, Valentín found himself near the top of the batting charts in Florida's Grapefruit League, hitting .405 with a handful of triples and twice as many doubles. Something had clicked for the man everyone respected and admired; the man that front offices always seemed to overlook on Opening Day. Aside from the sporadic call-ups during his career, surviving until the final round of Spring Training cuts often qualified as an achievement for the unassuming veteran from Mexico. After all, every day on the spring roster meant another opportunity to showcase his value to his team and to scouts around the league – and collect big league meal money. Valentín put his best effort forward every day he was afforded the opportunity to suit up and take the field. That one day he misses, he thought, could be the day someone might see something in him that they hadn't considered before. This spring, despite his short stature and unassuming demeanor, Valentín's performance was proving difficult for anyone to overlook.

After a few more rounds, Valentín clapped his palms together and called off the drill. Brashear mopped his face with his shirtsleeve and met his mentor with an appreciative fist bump. It's not every day that a 21-year-old kid gets a one-on-one fielding clinic from a defensive dynamo.

"Thanks for working with me, Val."

"Anytime, amigo. You've got it in you, I'm just trying to pull it out." He wrapped an arm around the young man's neck and yanked him toward the tunnel that led to the clubhouse. Brashear was as polished as they come at the plate and possessed all the attributes the demanding middle infield positions required. Despite a few hiccups during Valentín's drills, he had quick feet, soft hands, and was building a reputation in the minors as one of the strongest defenders on the Phillies' Triple-A affiliate, if not its entire minor league system. The organization hoped that a full spring regimen with Valentín would prepare him well for a future at second base, across the infield from Cuban sensation Jose Alvarez.

That, of course, was a double-edged sword for Valentín. Brashear's continued success served as a threat to his own status within the organization. To his credit, Valentín tried not to look at it that way. His roster status had always been perilous, his baseball mortality always on the precipice. Whether it was at the plate, in the field, or as the resident fount of knowledge for eager young ballplayers, he was at peace with his role. If he could extend his career as a player or accelerate his transition to the next stage as a coach, he'd do whatever was asked of him and do it to the best of his abilities. That's why, with a couple weeks left in spring training, he remained in camp. And whether he realized it or not, he was making it harder and harder for the Phillies' brass to do what most expected they would do: thank him for his work and then cut him loose to latch on with yet another farm squad in search of veteran leadership. In fact, the debate surrounding Valentín was centered on how valuable that veteran leadership might be on the big league club.

"How'd he do?" McGown's voice stopped Valentín mid-stride as he passed the manager's office. "I saw you working with Brashear."

"He's a good kid. He'll do well here." Valentín crossed his arms and leaned against the doorframe, a familiar checkpoint for many ballplayers on the walk back to the clubhouse from the practice fields. He was always at ease with coaches, perhaps because they often treated him like one of their own rather than a role player hanging on for dear life at the end of the bench. "You can slot him in today and he won't embarrass himself. He's only going to get better."

"I'd have to agree with you. Appreciate you putting in the time."

"That's why I'm here, Skipper. Whatever I can pass on to the young guys, you know that I'm happy to do it." Valentín meant it. Whereas McGown saw a little bit of himself in Valentín – always hustling, always working to get everything he could out of his abilities – Valentín saw a little bit of himself in every wide-eyed kid getting a taste of The Show for the first time. Some make it and stick, others don't. Valentín had enjoyed enough time in big league clubhouses and endured enough of the disappointment that comes with falling short, to appreciate the benefit of putting in the extra effort. He led by example, passed on whatever knowledge he possessed, and hoped at least a few of the young guys prospered because of it.

"You're here for much more than that," McGown set aside his paperwork, a stack of lineup cards for the next week's action, and approached his veteran infielder. "I hope you know that. We're going to need you this year, Marcel."

"I'll be ready for the call whenever it comes – you can count on it."

"That's the thing, Marcel. I know I can." McGown gave his reliable vet a rap on the shoulder and Valentín tipped his eyes toward the ground with a chuckle. "I'm counting on you to be ready on April 3."

A funny thing happened when those words reached Valentín's ears. If the hardest part of McGown's job was delivering bad news to hard-working guys who deserve better, the best part was manifesting before his eyes in the sterile corridor of the team's Spring Training complex.

"Opening Day..." His voice trailed off and his eyes welled. Opening Day. At 34 years of age, after more than a decade of heartbreak and shortfalls, Marcel Valentín would stand along the first base line with his teammates, hand over his heart, while "The Star-Spangled Banner" played before a sellout crowd. In the land of opportunity, he was finally finding his in Philadelphia.

"Opening Day. You earned this, Marcel. You earned it." McGown spoke in an earnest tone. He wanted to make certain that his most underappreciated and underrated player understood that his spot had not been gifted to him out of sympathy. "I've seen what you've done with regular playing time and we all recognize what you do with the young guys when everyone else steps away from the diamond. I can't promise you an everyday role, but I'll do my damnedest to keep you sharp."

"You can throw me in the bullpen if it means I'll see some action." The words came out with a quiver and both men laughed at the thought.

"You know, I just might do that. Careful what you wish for."

"Fourteen years, Skip. It took me 14 years and 11 camp invites to get this opportunity." Amid the laughter, it was Valentín's turn to be earnest. "I won't let you down."

"You never have. Just do what you've done down here – be a leader, set the tone – and I'll give you every opportunity to keep your spot."

Valentín thanked his manager a few more times before jogging down the ramp to join his teammates in the locker room. With trembling hands, he reached for his phone and placed the only call he could think of making at a moment like this.

"Bueno?"

"Mamá! Lo logré!" *I made it.*

After 14 years, he made it.

3

The Ace

After all these years, there was still nothing quite like that sound. For Aaron Tanner, little else matched the hiss of a baseball buzzing through the air, followed by the *thwack!* of contact with an outstretched catcher's mitt.

Once a baby-faced prospect, Tanner had grown into the role of staff ace in short order. Entering his fourth full season, success had come easy for the young hurler from West Texas and early prognostications tapped Tanner for big things at the age of 26. After improving his numbers each season, even registering among the top 10 in Cy Young Award voting the previous year, many experts expected Tanner to rise among the league's elite with a breakout season. Contending for a Cy Young Award was one thing, but Tanner was his own toughest critic: with sky-high expectations, he didn't just want to be a contender, he wanted to win the honor as the league's best pitcher. And on this day, as his teammates took turns trying, and failing, to make contact during an informal batting practice session, he certainly had the look of a pitcher destined for greatness.

It wasn't just the four-seam fastball, which touched 98 on a bad day and spilled from his fingertips effortlessly. It was how he could paint the black with his heater, and follow it up with a knee-buckling changeup that rarely cracked 80 miles-per-hour. The fact that both pitches followed a near identical path and left his hand at just about the same release point made the combination even more deadly. And if this late-March intra-squad session against live hitters, a final tune-up before the new season, was any indication, he had the look of a man ready to deliver on those mounting expectations.

"Save some bullets for Monday." A gruff voice shouted from behind the cage. "It's a long season; I don't need you hitting triple-digits in March."

Ever the voice of reason, Pedro Arroyo had served as the Phillies' pitching coach for the past eight seasons. In that role, his most important job was protecting his young arms from themselves. Tanner often tested the boundaries.

"I'm fired up. Itching to get started."

"Save some bullets." Arroyo repeated the order and Tanner acquiesced, kicking at the dirt in front of the dusty pitching rubber atop the mound.

"Fair enough. I'll save a few." For all his eagerness to let it fly, he appreciated the guardrails the old man set up for his protection. If left to his own devices, Tanner may have thrown his arm out by midday. That's just how he was wired. Ever since he was a kid, he loved the feel of a baseball in his hand. Even more, he loved the way it felt on its way out. From a young age, he would try to pinpoint the moment that the ball took flight, the last millisecond the stitches hung close to his fingertips before the ball surged toward its target. As a child, and as if he had been plucked from a storybook of baseball clichés, Tanner refined the art of pitching by playing catch with his father until sundown each night. Of course, it didn't even have to be a baseball: on the long walk to school each morning, Tanner would hurl every stone he could find at whatever target might come into view, every thrown stone serving as preparation for his future in baseball. Sure enough, he was a caricature of the big league dreamer, fantasizing about World Series heroics along dusty roads and on the sprawling fields of the family ranch. Flash-forward 15 years, and he was well on his way to making the fantasy a reality.

After a few more tosses, Tanner pulled his glove off and skipped from the mound to join a few teammates loitering behind the cage. Another successful romp through the Grapefruit League was in the books. For a ballplayer in Tanner's position – that is, a surefire ace with a guaranteed slot at the top of the starting rotation – the goal of Spring Training was always the same: stay healthy enough to take the mound when the games matter. Still, he couldn't help but try to dazzle the small Florida crowds and the swarm of analysts and talking heads that had predicted greatness. He had a flare for the dramatic and wasn't satisfied to merely "get his work in," as many of his teammates and players across the league often commented when reporters asked about spring performances. No, Tanner was more inclined to adopt another overplayed Spring Training interview trope, "I'm in the best shape of my life," and he was always more than happy to run out to the mound and prove it. So, when he touched 101 on the gun in early March one spring, it led to equal parts anger and awe: awe from the outsiders, the fans and the analysts, who had little riding on his able right shoulder. Anger from the Phillies' front office and coaching staff, all of whom had everything riding on the young man's continued success – and health. While Tanner learned his lesson quickly, he was good for at least one similar stunt each year when March rolled around again.

Six days separated Tanner from his first Opening Day start. He was the man in Philly and he knew it. He welcomed it and relished the opportunity to take his team and its fans to the Promised Land. That's what Aces do, he figured. He also had goals for himself and he planned to check the boxes one by one. Coming off a 16-win season, he wanted 20. The moment he struck out his two-hundredth batter in the previous season's final game, he set a goal to knock down another 50 the following season. His 187 innings, a steady and safe increase from the 168 he logged two years prior, weren't nearly enough. He wanted to finish games – so the goal was set for 225 innings and, despite pitching in an era of specialist relievers and carefully monitored pitch counts, he wanted to complete as many games as his manager would allow. Ever the team player, he figured he could help the bullpen get its rest by going as deep in games as he possibly could. His 2.60 earned run average? Well, that just wouldn't do. Tanner didn't see a reason to give up any runs at all, but figured sub-2.00 would be a reasonable target. Aside from his lofty personal goals, however, Tanner just wanted a World Series ring. And if he pitched the way he was capable of pitching, he saw no reason why Philadelphia couldn't celebrate Halloween with a World Championship parade through Center City.

"You looked good out there, sugar bear." Tanner snapped out of his daydreams to find his wife and the couple's three-year-old daughter leaning against the barricade just to the left of the dugout. "You gonna listen to Pedro this year?"

"I always listen, babe. I always listen." He kissed his wife, Jessica, a tiny thing with long brunette hair knotted in braids down to her shoulders, and launched his little pixie into the air amid gleeful squeals. "How's my big girl?"

"I sawed you throwing, dada." The little girl loved watching her father pitch, though the attention span of a toddler leaves much to be desired. "Can we go now? I'm hungry."

"Daddy has to wash up, but Momma can take you back home." Tanner passed Ella back to her mother and kissed her on the forehead. "You get on back to the condo. I won't be long."

"Sounds good – I'll see you soon. Are you fixin' to nap or should we go to the b-e-a-c-h?" Jessica spelled out the word just in case a visit to Florida's nearby Gulf waters was not in the cards.

"Nah, baby, I won't be able to sleep – I'm wired. Besides, it's going to be cold in Philly – we need to get our beach time in while we can!" The little girl's ears perked up as her father said the magic word. They disappeared up the ramp toward the parking lot and he fell back into the routine of a big league ballplayer putting the final touches on a successful, uneventful spring. As much as he would miss the comforts of low-key West Florida, he couldn't wait to stand on that mound in Philadelphia – to see his breath pour out into the chilly night air and feel the wave of noise from 45,000 fans after the long and quiet winter. Nothing compared and he was ready for the journey to begin anew.

4

Tough Decisions

"Which way are you leaning?" Phillies' General Manager Mark Johnson, hands clasped behind his head, studied the white board that hung above the desk of John McGown. In black marker, 28 names were scribbled across two columns that represented both a mostly complete roster of 26 players making the trip to Philadelphia and two tough decisions. The left side of the white board featured the names of those who would head north when the team departed its home away from home in two days. You didn't want to be on the other list.

"I like Bennett. I like a lefty who can rear back and blow people away," McGown tapped a pen against his teeth as he examined each name on the board. "That's a rare combination."

"Track record is a little suspect." Johnson was a realist. While McGown saw marked improvement in Bennett Peterson's control, his Achilles' heel during an up-and-down big league career, Johnson harbored a reasonable amount of fear that regression to the norm might be just ahead once the team returned to the bright lights of regular season baseball. "How much do you trust him with a runner on base late in the game?"

21

"I trust him. I think he turned a corner, I really do." McGown thought back to his conversation with the big lefty a few weeks earlier. A bundle of nerves at that time, hanging onto the big league dream and flailing, Peterson seemed like a different player today. In 19 spring innings he had struck out 26 men and allowed only three free passes. Of course, numbers amassed during meaningless exhibition games are best taken with a grain of salt. Given the circumstances, however, McGown felt that Peterson's numbers meant just a little bit more than usual: the product of a desperate man making one final push for what might be his last chance to reach his full potential. Ever the optimist, McGown wanted to believe Peterson's success would carry over. "It's a tough call to make, especially given what Smith did for us down the stretch last season."

"He was terrific." Johnson allowed his thoughts to drift to Paul Smith's clutch performances in August and September during the previous season. Well out of contention by July, the Phillies' fortunes might have taken an even worse turn had it not been for the performance of the crafty lefty during a few late season ballgames. And now, in the final days of Spring Training, Smith and Peterson had arrived at the same place: in between a roster spot and the unknown. Peterson had built his reputation on power and unfulfilled potential. So, keeping him in the mix would equate to placing a bet on that potential. Would this be the year he managed to harness the full scope of his abilities? Or would he again lose track of his mechanics and flame out?

Smith, on the other hand, was the model of modest, under-the-radar consistency. Profiling as little more than middle relief help, that's all he ever needed to be. He was a soft-tossing lefty who didn't miss too many bats, but Smith managed to get the job done well enough to survive nine years in The Show. Spring baseball, however, had not been kind to the veteran. His fastball, if you could call it that, barely topped 80 and for the first time in his career, he struggled to locate his pitches. When you hit triple digits on the radar gun, you can get away with an occasional misfire. Smith, on the other hand, lived and died with his ability to paint the corners and place his pitches in *just* the right spot. He had been exposed during Spring Training and had the look of a pitcher who might not fool anyone anymore. Again, the mantra of taking Spring Training numbers with a grain of salt rang loudly in the minds of Johnson and McGown as they deliberated. However, it's hard to overlook abject failure – even in those meaningless exhibitions.

"I hate to rely on what he did this spring, but there is something to it and I know what I saw." McGown turned to his GM, who appeared to age before his eyes as they continued with the agonizing and exhausting debate. "His velocity is down, he can't locate, and I'm just not sure he's going to get guys out anymore. It's a tough call, but I'd like to see what Peterson can do with a real opportunity."

"Listen, in the end, it's your call." The GM put his hands in the air before leaning across the table toward McGown. "It comes down to who you feel comfortable handing the ball to when it matters most. That's what I want for this ball club – I trust your judgment and I'll support whatever decision you want to make here."

"It's Peterson for me."

"Then it's Peterson." Johnson stood and moved toward the door. "These are hard decisions to make. In the end, you know you have my support."

McGown didn't look away from the board while his GM slipped into the hallway. He reached for the eraser, removed a name, and rewrote "Peterson" along the left-hand side. The hard-throwing lefty would get his opportunity to prove he had what it took to make it through the long big league season. In the meantime, McGown had another hard conversation ahead of him. Paul Smith would catch on somewhere, McGown rationalized. He had a respectable track record and, in this league, that meant something. Probably one more deal, hopefully with a guarantee. Many soft-tossing lefties with less skill than Smith made a decent living playing out their final years on a series of one-year deals. He imagined Smith wouldn't be out of work long.

"Paul, can you pop in for a minute?" The unassuming lefty looked up from his shoes to find his manager calling to him from across the clubhouse. "It'll just take a sec."

While the game of baseball is unpredictable, there are still a few instances in a ballplayer's career that are telegraphed perfectly. It's unavoidable. This was one of those moments for Paul Smith. Late in Spring Training, as an under-performing veteran with a penchant for coming up big in the biggest spots, you try to navigate the turmoil as best you can. Before each outing, you hope for improvement, and when it doesn't come, you hope the coaching staff had seen enough of your body of work to know what you would bring to the ball club. For Smith, however, his precipitous decline wasn't a matter of bad luck or a missed pitch here or there. He knew it and he recognized that the coaching staff knew it too. He saw it in their faces when his fastball barely broke 80 on the gun. He watched their body language when minor league retreads crushed his offerings all over the field. He wasn't injured, but something was broken.

"Sure thing, Mac." Smith jogged to his manager, and both men walked together in silence, interrupted by the rattling of cleats on the cement floor. His heart beat out of his chest in anticipation of what was coming. After months of frustration and missed opportunity, it was time to face reality.

"How's the arm, Paul?" McGown closed the door of his office and the two men faced one another across his desk.

"I feel great. Haven't felt this good in years." Smith looked down and shook his head with disgust. "I almost wish I had a different answer for you."

"How's that?"

"I'd just like to have some answers, is all. Something to explain..." He trailed off and turned his eyes toward the fluorescent lights buzzing overhead. Tears formed in the corners of his eyes and he hoped his manager hadn't noticed.

"Been a tough spring, Paul."

"It sure has."

"The numbers aren't good. You're a grown man and I'm going to tell it to you straight because you don't need me blowing smoke. You gave it your all this spring – I know that," McGown tried to offer his steady veteran something – anything – to boost his confidence. "You battled. That's all I ask of you guys."

"I appreciate that. I sure as hell tried to get on track."

"I know you did." McGown took a deep breath and Smith could feel the hammer coming down. "Paul, we had to make a hard choice here. You won't be heading north with us."

For both men, inevitability didn't make the moment any easier. Smith had been a roster lock for several seasons, but when it goes, it goes fast. McGown, on the other side of the table, was making a choice that impacted lives – that's a hard position to be in, but it came with the job.

"Damn. I guess I didn't give you much to work with, did I?" Smith's words were measured as he tried to keep his emotions in check. "Who's coming up?"

"We're going with Peterson."

"Peterson. Good." McGown sensed the relief in the man's response. "I'm glad it's him. Talk about battling."

"We think he found something," McGown said. "We think he earned a shot to prove us right."

McGown watched Smith scan the room one final time. At times like this, it was easy to become nostalgic about every nook and cranny of the old spring complex. When you're cut loose in pro ball, you never know when or if another opportunity might come.

"You're out of minor league options, as I'm sure you know." McGown wanted to leave Smith with a sense of hope that his situation would improve with haste. "So we can't hide you in the minors without exposing you to waivers, which we'll do. The minor league life isn't for you anyway – you deserve better."

"How do you see it playing out?" As much as Smith would have liked to stick with the Phillies, a big league job sure beat the bus life of the bush leagues. "It hasn't been easy for me this spring, I know that. But I know I can still compete; I've still got that fire in me."

"From the outside looking in, other teams can make a few educated guesses about how our roster might shake out and who might be available." Smith leaned forward with interest, wiping moisture from his eyes in spite of himself. "The Cubs will have the first crack at you on the waiver wire and they've let on that they're in the market for a guy who can come in and knock down a tough lefty. I'd like to think they'll place a claim on you once you've been DFA'd. Maybe we'll see you at Wrigley this season."

Smith cracked a smile. Maybe this wasn't one of those perfectly telegraphed moments after all. McGown, it appeared, was full of surprises.

"I can still do that, you know." Smith looked right at his manager as his eyes filled with moisture once again. "I can still get that one out in a tough spot. Wish I did it for you more often this spring, but I know I can still get the job done."

"I'm sure that's what Mark will tell them. You'd do well there, Paul. I know you'll do great anywhere you land." McGown cleared his throat and broke eye contact. He wasn't one to get emotional at times like this, but Paul Smith was one of the good guys in the game and though he wouldn't admit it, McGown was going to miss handing the ball to him.

"I loved pitching in Philadelphia, truly. I'm grateful for opportunities I've had to pitch in that city." Smith made his home in Center City and had made the city his adopted home since the team acquired him from Baltimore several years earlier. He grew up in Iowa, however, and a return to the Midwest would represent a homecoming of sorts.

"I know you do. And you've given us all you could – let's see how the next few days play out." McGown didn't want to make any promises he couldn't keep. Not to a guy like Smith; it just wouldn't be fair. "If it's not the Cubs, I can't imagine you'll be out of work long."

Smith stood to leave and shook McGown's hand. He had thrown his final pitch for the Phillies, but left the office encouraged that, if the chips fell the right way, perhaps he still had a few big league bullets left.

"Peterson in the clubhouse?" As one door closed, another would open.

"Sure is."

"Can you send him in?"

Evening shadows were getting longer and the sun was setting on another slate of spring exhibitions – meaningless to some, but not to those who need every chance they could get to show their stuff, to prove they belong. Now that some decisions had been made, McGown and his GM would start the next day before sunrise to make one final, excruciating decision about the future of two more grown men living on the bubble. Not tonight, however. Tonight, he would end on a high note and reward a young man who truly belonged.

5

Road to Redemption

"You wanted to see me, Mac?" Peterson filled the door-way and fidgeted like he wanted to be anywhere else but in his manager's office. The reliever had seen this movie before, and it never ended well. Not for him, at least. McGown chuckled and motioned his big, bearded hurler toward a chair.

"Take a seat." There's a time-honored tradition of tomfoolery that comes with informing a player he'd be pitching with the big club once the league concludes its Spring Training schedule. McGown liked a good rib as much as anyone, but more often, he played it straight. Especially with a sensitive type like Peterson; he figured it might be best to let the man just enjoy his moment. In a career filled with roadblocks, making the team out of Spring Training promised to rank among his career highlights to that point. McGown hoped it was just the beginning.

"You've had a nice spring."

"Something clicked for me, I feel real confident in my stuff right now, Mac." Peterson wriggled as much as the chair would allow beneath his weight. Nervous energy, even now. Even after the most productive run of his life.

"You should feel that way," McGown replied. "Think you can keep it going when the games matter?"

"I know I can."

"Me too." McGown extended a hand, which was promptly swallowed up by his new lefty. "Congratulations, son. You're in my 'pen. This ain't a gift; you've earned it."

"Thank you, Mac. I won't let you down." Peterson's chair rattled across the floor, startling him as he stood. He had the look of a man ready to explode.

"I know you won't. Remember: deep breath, let it fly. Not a lefty in this league you can't punch out."

"I'll be ready anytime you make the call," Peterson said as he disappeared down the hall. He couldn't get out of McGown's office fast enough – no sense giving the old manager a chance to change his mind.

As McGown settled back into his chair to wrap up a few loose ends, he heard the clang of footsteps running down the hall followed by a primal roar. He let out a laugh at Peterson's release. After sharing the good news with his newest bullpen weapon, McGown figured it was only a matter of time before that pent-up energy spilled over. Already high-strung and jumpy, if Peterson felt the need to punctuate his promotion with a few hearty roars, well, that would do just fine.

"Hello?"

The woman on the other end of the line answered with a whisper. While most were wide-awake at this time of day, a stay-at-home mom catches a few moments of rest whenever her toddler allows. If that means a late-afternoon nap, so be it.

"I'm sorry, honey. Did I wake you?" Peterson had calmed himself after his hallway outburst. Alone once again in that very same dimly lit echo chamber of cement, the first call he would make was one he had been waiting to make his entire career in pro ball.

"It's okay. Julie finally went down. What time is it?"

"Almost five."

"Huh. Well, that's good. She's been out for an hour then." Abagail paused, perhaps realizing he may have news, for better or worse. Perhaps not for any reason at all. You never can tell as this stage of Spring Training. "How was your day?"

"Another day at the office. I had a good session this morning – sure feels like it's all coming together." Peterson was bursting at the seams. At the same time, he wanted the moment to last; after so many disappointments, he wanted to savor her reaction, something he had been waiting for his entire playing career. After all, Peterson had always felt as though his success on the field was now and always had been hers as much as it was his own.

College sweethearts, Abigail and Bennett met during Welcome Week at Tulane and the rest was history. While he left after his junior year when the Mets made him a third-round selection, she graduated with a degree in early childhood development and hopped from one school district to another into her mid-twenties depending on his minor league assignments. She never hesitated to embrace the nomadic life that came with chasing the big league dream – a chase that became more treacherous as the years passed and teams grew impatient with the unfulfilled potential wasting away in Peterson's left arm. Abigail was an army brat, and as such she received more training than most people to prepare herself for the humble realities of life between the major and minors, bracing herself every time the phone rang. Sometimes, it was a call-up to the majors. Sometimes, an assignment in a nearby city. Sometimes, the news was much worse.

"They must be getting pretty close to making decisions. Whatever they decide, we'll make it work, Ben."

"I know we will." He couldn't take it any longer. He didn't have much of a poker face and he was pretty sure she'd hear the excitement in his voice before too long. "Have you given any thought to what neighborhood you might like if it works out in Philly?"

"Aaron's wife gave me a few good suggestions, but don't worry about that, baby. You concentrate on camp." He could feel the tears forming. She was so strong, so even keeled. "We'll be happy wherever we are."

"You might want to schedule some open houses."

"Bennett! *Bennett Peterson!!* Did you get the call?" Now it was her time to share in the excitement. Abigail was always a steadying presence for him through the ups and downs. He wanted her to enjoy their moment just as much as he had.

"I made it, Abby. We're going to Philly!"

"Ben, I'm so proud of you! You worked so hard for this." In the background, he could hear his little girl toddling over to her mother to see what all the commotion was about. All it took was a reminder about the team's mascot, the iconic Philly Phanatic, for Julie to share in her parents' delight. When you're not quite three years old, it's the little things that deliver the most pleasure.

"It's been a tough road, but I think we've turned a corner," he said. "I'd like to think this is our last move for a while. I'm going to keep grinding so we can make Philly home. That's what you deserve."

"I love you."

"I love you too, Abby."

"Come on home, let's celebrate."

———

McGown shut off the light to his office and, like most nights, walked in silence across the practice field to his car. He enjoyed the quiet, the moment of reflection that followed another taxing day. Toward the end of March, that's how it always worked. For top stars, the final days of the exhibition slate are easy: take a few at-bats, get a little field work in, and keep the excitement of a new season in check. For the team's chief decision-makers, McGown and Johnson in particular, the final days before a new season were wrought with agonizing, unavoidable decisions to firm up final roster spots. To be sure, not every decision was difficult for the same reason. McGown had grown attached to a few of his players through the years and it's always just a little bit harder to let someone go when you've become close. More often, however, it was a fear of making a mistake that made roster cuts so difficult. Right or wrong, the team's architects must live with the outcome of their decisions. Not all players pass through waivers unclaimed. Not all outright cuts bomb out in their next city. Sometimes, when making personnel decisions, mistakes are made and every now and then, those ghosts come back to haunt you.

McGown was ready to get back to Philadelphia, but nights like this, cooled by a steady breeze blowing east across the Gulf of Mexico, offered a sense of peace and stillness that was hard to find during the daylight hours – let alone anywhere near the ballpark back home. His Grapefruit League experience reminded him of the minor league grind and unlike most of his managerial brethren, McGown couldn't help but look back with pride and nostalgia. When he was working his way up the chain as a young ballplayer, the long bus trips never bothered him. Each was a chance to see the country from a new perspective, a chance to explore the America that long-time big leaguers tend to forge: the unassuming Main Street business districts, the rolling hills, and fields of ripening harvests. In some ways, the short Spring Training road trips across the Sunshine State offered faint reminders of the game's roots. Players rode the bus from one beach town to another and plied their craft in small ballparks filled with low-key crowds. As much as McGown loved and appreciated the benefits of big league life, Coastal Florida suited him just fine. Alone with his thoughts but for the rhythmic patter of sprinklers springing to life on the field just behind him, the solitude helped McGown reset and clear his mind for another day, his final day, at the team's Spring Training complex. After that, a summer in Philadelphia awaited. A season of promise, of slowly heightening expectations, would begin with his young Ace, Aaron Tanner, hoping to set the tone.

6

Life on the Road

Marcus Cooper was a long way from home.

Somewhere along the dusty border of the continental U.S. and Mexico, somewhere between the tumbleweeds of South Texas and the middle of nowhere, Cooper sat in the sun behind a rusted backstop and watched a couple dozen kids play baseball.

It was more complex than that, of course. As he settled into the veritable broiler where he would bake for the next two to three hours, Cooper kept his eyes trained on one or two of those Texas boys playing catch and running drills. Sammy Pinto, a 17-year-old first baseman and a recommendation from one of his trusted area scouts, took a few tosses from his third baseman and rifled the ball around the infield during warm-ups. Built like a fire hydrant, the senior was destined for... something. At this stage, in this place, it was hard to say for sure where his path would lead. But that was the challenge for guys like Cooper: find a guy with ability and project his development as best you can. After watching the young man play in this sleepy town for the past few days, Cooper had seen enough in Pinto to keep him on the board: maybe a late pick, maybe somewhere after the twentieth round. If he was still available after twenty rounds, Cooper imagined it might be worth sticking a guy like Pinto in rookie ball to see if he had what it takes.

A few feet away from Pinto stood Ronald Jasper, a lanky left-handed pitcher still growing into his body. He stood well over six feet, maybe closer to six-and-a-half feet tall. Jasper would be celebrating his eighteenth birthday in a few days, but aside from his height, you wouldn't have known it by looking at him. Clean-shaven with big brown eyes, he had an aloof, childlike demeanor that made him appear more than a couple years younger. That youthful disposition distracted from the anxiety Jasper kept just below the surface; the inner critic who was sometimes his own worst enemy. Pinto was a good old boy who forgot his at-bats the moment he left the batter's box, and seldom dwelled on what the future might hold. Jasper, on the other hand, was quite the opposite.

Growing up just outside of El Paso, Texas, Jasper had moved with his family to this one-horse town in Jeff Davis County a few years back and watched his big league dream die along with the move. For as long as he could remember, he wanted to play baseball. In El Paso, playing in one of the state's premier baseball programs, someone might take notice of the towering left-hander lighting up the radar gun and whirling around the mound with a wiry, deceptive delivery. He was all arms and legs and it worked. No one would find him here, he feared. And for the most part, he was right.

Cooper had heard about Jasper's exploits the way many scouts find out about small town stars who might project as raw, but moldable – and draft-able – talent: He watched a lot of baseball games. This visit, coming at the tail end of his latest tour through West and South Texas, was his first opportunity to see Jasper take the mound in a full year. Of course, even this encounter hadn't been a certainty. With so many ball games on his schedule – so many towns to visit, so many players to analyze – lining up his visit with starts by the pitchers he intended to study came with a higher degree of difficulty. When he knew the coaches well, and through the years he had gotten to know his fair share, sometimes he'd place a few calls to announce his arrival quietly to those he trusted. He never wanted the young athletes to know ahead of time that their next games might be played under the watchful eye of a Major League scout. After all, if he wanted an honest performance out of his targets, it was best to let the kids play ball rather than try to put on a show. On game day, it wouldn't take long for most of the boys to figure out that the old man with a notepad and radar gun might be a scout. If he had his druthers, however, he preferred to keep his presence discreet. That was especially true of Jasper, a young man who spun himself up to such a degree each time he pitched that knowledge of Cooper's presence might have been his undoing.

On this day in April, the stars aligned. Cooper, whose presence remained unannounced, would have a bird's eye view of the young man who was the talk of a town that nobody talked about. And, as it would turn out, his impressions of the stocky first baseman would improve, too.

"Hey, Coop. Whaddya say?" Cooper looked up to find Finn Breslin, an area supervisor for the Minnesota Twins, shuffling toward him along the bleacher bench one step up from where he sat. "Phillies bringing out the big guns for these boys, eh?"

"I try to make the rounds, Finn. How else am I going to run into you these days?" Cooper reached for a handshake and smiled. "It's good to see you – you coming or going?"

"It's a new day and a new trip." Breslin took a seat just behind Cooper's shoulder and applied a healthy amount of sunscreen beneath the bill of his hat and on his exposed neck. In these parts, even in April, there was no such thing as too much sunscreen. "I'll be on the road for the next three weeks."

"Wouldn't have it any other way, Finn. I don't know what to do with myself in the office," Cooper replied. As the Phillies scouting director, he could pick and choose his trips. Forty years in the game provided slightly more schedule flexibility than he had enjoyed as a pup just starting out. Still, he preferred baking in the sun while watching a few long shots play ball over sitting in the office any day of the week.

Cooper and Breslin stood out among the fans that made up the small South Texas crowd. Amid cheers and chants from the family and friends that joined the two old scouts on the creaky bleacher bench, murmurs bubbled up from time to time as fans guessed who they might represent and more importantly, who they were watching. In this small town, on this rutted baseball diamond, it wasn't hard to figure out the second part based on performance alone. Pinto hit a couple of Little League home runs – that is, the inside-the-park variety where the ball rolls into the distance forever, unobstructed because of the field's lack of an outfield fence. He also showed surprising efficiency at first base, moving from side to side with the kind of grace one can only discover on trips such as this. While Cooper jotted down a few notes about Pinto's movement to the ball and above-average instincts, a wry smile creased his lips. In an era of scouting that involved more data scientists and statistical analysis than ever before, this game showed the value of having scouts deployed in the field. Baseball analytics hadn't quite figured out the perfect formula to quantify instincts yet.

"That boy right there's got some ability," Breslin had commented after one of Pinto's big flies. "I don't see a big leaguer, but he can swing the stick."

The star of the show, of course, was Jasper. A bundle of nerves since tipping 90 miles per hour with his first pitch, his constant movement and chaotic delivery couldn't distract from the fact that somewhere beneath the mayhem, somewhere beneath the tangle of arms and legs, was a damn fine pitcher. Even when he realized that he was pitching for an audience of scouts, it didn't detract from his performance. After a six-inning outing of shutout ball and a pile of strikeouts, Jasper exited the game in line for a win and visited quietly with his parents along the first base line. Cooper imagined that with proper coaching, maybe the young man could keep his mechanics in check. And if he did that, who knows how far he could go with that electric left arm? That's the big question every scout faces, however. Who knows? In baseball, there are few sure things and for as good as Jasper appeared to be, he was the furthest thing from it. Even with two scouts in attendance, even with Cooper and Breslin both watching the same talent, there were no guarantees either would wind up recommending the tall lefty to their respective organizations. Both scouts saw talent, but there was talent on the diamond in every high school game. During the season, even with his reduced schedule, Cooper would watch thousands of high schoolers play baseball across the U.S. Jasper was far from a finished product and far from the top of the list. What Jasper didn't know was that if he wasn't at the top, he was also nowhere near the bottom.

After the game, Cooper and Breslin shook hands and headed toward the parking lot. Cooper would head to the airport and back to Philadelphia while Breslin continued his journey of small-town baseball fields across Texas and into Oklahoma. Both men left with strong impressions of Ronald Jasper. As a bonus for Cooper, Sammy Pinto had opened his eyes as well. Neither scout compared notes, though it was safe to assume that Jasper's name would be on both of their lists during the upcoming draft after the more celebrated amateur standouts fell off the board. No one would mistake Jasper for an early pick – too raw, too much uncontrolled body movement. Even after just a couple encounters, Cooper recognized that the kid might also be too much of an over-thinker to make it in pro ball. But in the twelfth round? Thirteenth? Why not take a flier on a talent with a few flaws? Some flaws can be corrected. Others may not matter at all. Cooper figured that while no one would say two words about the kid on draft day, he might be the kind of player everyone in Philadelphia would be talking about six years down the road. All part of a day's work for Marcus Cooper and his scouts. Wherever Jasper ended up, selected by Philadelphia or another team, Cooper would make a note to check back a few years down the road to see if his hunch proved correct.

7

Struggles

Aaron Tanner sat in front of his locker, a doorless closet filled with pressed dress shirts, jerseys, and a collection of baseballs along the edge of a shelf, each representing firsts. Opening Day, an afternoon tilt against the visiting Chicago Cubs, represented a first of a different kind, but he didn't want to hang onto any mementos to mark the occasion. The Cubs jumped him for three first-inning runs and built a seven-run lead by the fourth inning when McGown made the call to the bullpen and lifted his talent-rich star. It was the first time in Tanner's short career that he failed to finish the fourth inning and he would be lying if he said it didn't bother him. On this day, however, his team got him off the hook.

Expected to be a decent, not great, offense, the Phillies scored runs in bunches and pulled away late, bringing home a 12-9 win in the Opening Day slugfest. An eighth inning pinch-hit grand slam from journeyman infielder Marcel Valentín, an unlikely source of power, proved to be the deciding blow. Valentín then turned in the defensive play of the night in the ninth when, as a defensive replacement at second base, he ranged to his right on a ball destined for the outfield and recorded the game's final out with a dive and a toss to shortstop Jose Alvarez for the force out at second. Who knew what untold damage awaited had he missed that ball, which would have plated two runs with the Cubs' biggest threat scheduled to bat next? When the game ended, Tanner was the first man out of the dugout to offer his appreciation to the savvy veteran. Now, alone with his thoughts in a room filled with people, he couldn't help but reflect on what went wrong.

A few minutes before the team's beat writers poured through the doors, the clubhouse environment delivered what you might expect following an Opening Day victory. Loud music – a blend of hip-hop and Latin-inspired pop songs – filled the air, which was humid on account of the scalding water rushing from a dozen shower heads. Conversation, animated and excited, soared over the music in fits and starts. Southern twang blended with various Spanish dialects to create a cornucopia of spoken word and laughter. For the team, with one win in the books and 161 more games to go, life was good.

"Alright, men. We're opening the doors. Let's get this show on the road so we can get home." McGown turned away from his team to begin the preparations for the next night's game in his office. Having already delivered his postgame press conference, the manager's public responsibilities would now transfer to his players while he turned his attention to the private, strategic responsibilities that come with the job. Through the years, McGown had developed a strong relationship with a few of the team's beat writers – not everyone, just a few that he trusted – the men and women who showed a little weariness beneath their eyes from life on the road, and a little less exuberance than the new wave of press box scribes. Life in baseball wears you down. McGown maintained an unspoken respect for anyone willing to put aside other pursuits to walk the winding path of a big league season year after year. And to his credit, he was always good for a few solid sound bites to make the unforgiving and thankless grind of following the team from city to city beneath the pressures of relentless deadlines worth the effort. He contemplated who they might gravitate to for their storytelling needs. Surely Alvarez, the flashy Cuban shortstop who made his big league debut and delivered with a three-hit night. Valentín earned himself a story or two as well, thanks to his clutch, game-deciding hit off the bench in his first Opening Day appearance. Of course, McGown's ace, Aaron Tanner, promised to be the star of the post-game show for all the wrong reasons after the worst outing of his career. The young man had poise, but would he crack amid the poking and prodding from the team's beat writers? No, that didn't sound like Tanner at all. *He'll turn the page quickly on this one*, he thought. *Get after it tomorrow.*

———

"Not the result you wanted tonight, but can you take us through your outing?"

"I just couldn't locate with my fastball." Tanner stood before a circle of reporters and spoke into several microphones and recording devices pointed toward his face. "All there is to it. They tattooed a few mistakes early and before you know it, you're staring at a crooked number."

"It's your first Opening Day assignment. Do you think nerves or excitement might have played a role?"

"Not at all. You know me – cool as a cucumber." He smiled. The beat writers laughed. After a tough night, a little laughter goes a long way toward moving on. "Like I said, I didn't have command of my fastball early. I'll get back to work tomorrow and I'd imagine the results will be better next time."

"What did you think of Valentín's at-bat?"

43

"He was awesome. The consummate pro – really bailed me out today." Tanner peeked over his shoulder at the hero of the day, also surrounded by reporters after his first Opening Day appearance. The young ace couldn't help but smile. "You feel good for a guy like that."

On a night like this, Tanner much preferred the conversation drift to the heroics of his veteran teammate. Ever agreeable and always polite with the press, Tanner still dreaded these encounters. The deconstruction of a miserable pitching performance is unpleasant any way you slice it.

"Can you tell me about the pitch you threw to Amora in the second?" Tanner was always amazed by the specificity of the questions. The questions always came after each of his starts, but the answers didn't change all that much.

"Which one, the slider?"

"I think it was a sinker. The one he hit for a double."

"It was a slider. It didn't slide." If it had been a sinker, he would have commented that it didn't sink. Such was the nature of these postgame discussions. When he had his best stuff working, he was nearly unhittable. Everybody knew that. When he didn't? The ball flattened out, usually high. Nothing more hittable than a high, straight pitch – a batting practice meatball. "It was working well for me this spring. Just one of those nights."

A few more questions and then the press pool shuffled together toward their next subject, the Cuban import with an interpreter stationed by his side, hands clasped behind his back. Tanner adjusted the ice wrap strapped to his shoulder beneath an unbuttoned dress shirt and turned to face his locker. *Just one of those nights*, he had said. In five days' time, he'd have the chance to show everyone that there was no cause for alarm. An electric performance in his second start would prove that the trendy Cy Young pick remained right on schedule. In the meantime, he would heed the advice of every coach and every savvy veteran starter who had tried to help the youngster move on from the occasional bomb in the past: try to forget. In the big leagues, it pays to have a touch of amnesia. When you're staring up at the bright lights with a 17.18 (*17.18!*) earned run average staring back at you, it's easier said than done. In a long season, however, Tanner understood how quickly fortunes change.

"Stop thinking about it." Tanner snapped out of his daze to find Pitching Coach Pedro Arroyo hovering above his shoulder. "You're thinking about it. Stop thinking about it."

"Just going over the mistakes. Trying to learn from them."

"You had no movement. It happens." Arroyo was a man of few words, but when he spoke up, everyone paid just a bit more attention. "You looked good in the pen, you'll look good next time you're back out on the bump. You'll make yourself crazy if you overanalyze every shitty pitch."

"I guess I can try to shut it down for the night." He paused to reflect on his reply. Truth was, he always had a hard time shutting it down. The young man's mind always worked overtime. "It's hard for me, you know. I want to be the best."

"And you'll get there the moment you turn your brain off after a start like that. Just go out there and pitch. The results will come." Arroyo slapped Tanner on the back and walked away. As polished as he had been at every stage of his professional journey, Tanner attributed the lion's share of his recent success to the old man. When he learned of his first All-Star nod, he made sure to offer gratitude to Arroyo first above all others. The man had helped him refine raw talent and transformed him from the thrower he was as a rookie into the pitcher he had become. On a rough night, there was no one else who could keep him grounded quite like Arroyo.

Collecting a few loose ends, Tanner moved past the dwindling crowds and out of the clubhouse. The doors closed behind him, and with quick goodbyes to a handful of stragglers milling about in the hallway, he jogged to the idling car waiting to bring him home after a tough night. Sliding into the passenger's seat, Tanner gave his wife a quick kiss and smiled at his daughter, sleeping peacefully in her car seat. Life is different for the child of a professional baseball player, to be sure. Ella would see more baseball by her fourth birthday than most people see in a lifetime. Some of his teammates kept their children home, which was occasionally clear across the country, and sometimes, beyond U.S. borders altogether. Together with his wife Jessica, Tanner had prioritized keeping the family as close as possible. In pro sports, you can go months without seeing family and that's a lifestyle the young man didn't want. The little girl had seen some late nights, and that would probably change once she started school. For now, however, seeing her little round face at the end of a rough performance helped put the highs and lows of big league life in perspective. He squeezed Jessica's thigh, closed his eyes, and thought of brighter days ahead.

"Let's go home," Tanner said, and drifted off to sleep.

8

Quiet Moments

"Can you pass the syrup?" Barrett Taylor, the Phillies' starting first baseman, reached across the greasy table to take a hand-off from his breakfast companion and counterpart on the other side of the diamond, third baseman Raul Valencia. "Thank you, kindly."

Taylor had spent the better part of three seasons mashing homers and snagging throws in the dirt from the talented, yet still developing Valencia. Batting fourth and fifth in the Phillies' lineup, they represented the team's biggest home run threats and they often delivered. For all his skill at the plate, however, Valencia remained a work-in-progress at the hot corner. He had transitioned from catcher to third base a few seasons earlier, and it was a move that came with its share of ups and downs. While an erratic throwing arm still revealed itself from time to time, the front office saw enough improvement in the Venezuelan to allow him to learn his new position on the job.

The calendar had turned to May and the weather in Philadelphia, while still unpredictable, was heating up. And following a slow start, the team's slugging duo hat hit their stride as well. On this day, which began with a pancake breakfast at a chain diner somewhere on the outskirts of Denver, the two men reflected on the first month of action before kicking off the first leg of a four-city, 10-game road trip. After enjoying an April schedule largely centered in Philadelphia with a few nearby road trips, the pendulum had swung the other way. The West Coast beckoned following a three-game set in Denver.

"What did you see in Dansby last night that I missed?" Taylor addressed Valencia between bites. Okay, during bites. "I couldn't hit him worth a damn."

"Guessed right on a changeup." Valencia, far more polite than his companion, waited to swallow before speaking. He found Taylor's lack of social graces endearing and together, they complemented one another's personalities well. "I was either going to look foolish or put us up by a couple runs. He's nasty."

"That rotation is going to be good for a long time. We've got some tough A-Bs ahead of us in Washington." Aside from his struggles against up-and-coming starter Kellen Dansby in the previous game, Taylor had put together a nice series against the Nationals' tough arms. Marred by a slow start to begin the new season, he went 8-18 in the four-game series with three home runs and a double, which helped the Phillies close out the month by taking three of four at home against their division rivals.

"It just felt good to get those runs back after that throw in the fourth," Valencia, ever the perfectionist, still stewed about an errant throw that led to a couple Nationals runs.

"The throws are getting better. That was your first error in what, five games? Six? You look more comfortable." Taylor would know. After all, he had a front row seat to what had been an adventure at times. The improvement was real, however, as Valencia's error count continued to decline, and the big first baseman didn't need to scoop quite as many throws out of the dirt as he had in past seasons.

"I feel more comfortable. It's getting easier every day."

"You can see it at the plate too. You're relaxed in the field and it's translating to other parts of your game." The parallel Taylor called out was not uncommon among his peers in baseball, and for Valencia, it had been even more pronounced. Starting the season with five errors during the first seven games, he also went hitless in his first 23 at-bats during that same stretch. Since then, he had hit .338 with six home runs and 20 runs batted in across the month's remaining 20 games. During that period, just a single misplay blemished his record. Both men hoped the trend would continue.

"Maybe so." For a short while, both men sat in silence amid the hum of the busy diner. The wait staff hustled from table to table, dropping off oversized heaps of pancakes or overstuffed omelets wherever they had been requested. The two ballplayers enjoyed their meal in relative obscurity save for the occasional double-take or pointed finger. Solid contributors if not superstars in Philadelphia, the heart of the Phillies' batting order remained mostly anonymous on the road.

"I like this tradition we have, you and me." Despite the break in conversation, Taylor couldn't be bothered to finish his bite before addressing Valencia, who only chuckled and shook his head.

"Pardon?"

"Breakfast. Starting our road trips with good food and good conversation." Taylor raised a finger in the air to catch the attention of a passing waiter. Valencia wouldn't have been surprised if his teammate planned to order another stack of pancakes, but instead, he motioned for the check. *A show of restraint*, he thought.

"Me too. A nice start to every trip." He folded his napkin across his plate and stretched. "What time are we supposed to be at Coors?"

"Two o'clock. I might head over a little early. Preston's gonna screw around a bit with a new drone." A sheepish grin revealed the excitement that Taylor was trying, and failing, to contain. He had big plans to spend the early afternoon hours testing the range of Preston Saunders' drone. "I'm gonna see what that baby can do. Maybe fly that thing over the top deck."

"You guys and your toys. Those things freak me out. I don't need blades that close to my fingers." Valencia shuddered for effect and the two men slid from the booth and toward the door. "I have enough trouble pickin' it at third."

Taylor laughed and draped a muscular arm around the shoulder of his third baseman, and his best friend. "Fair enough, Raul. Reason enough to stay away."

Bellies full of food with questionable nutritional value (but plenty of calories they would need for fuel), Valencia and Taylor disappeared down the block to catch a few winks at the hotel before turning their focus to a new month of baseball. One month in the books and Philadelphia sat within striking distance of the division-leading New York Mets, a game-and-a-half behind at 17-10. It was a strong start for a team on the rise, leaving many to wonder just how good they could be as the season wore on. And, how good they might be if their ace, Aaron Tanner, got himself on track.

———

"The biggest disappointment for the surprising Phillies has to be, without a doubt, the performance of Aaron Tanner." Tanner sat by himself in the visiting clubhouse watching two blowhards tear him apart on a cable sports program. He arrived at the ballpark early, as he often did, in order to run several sets of stairs along the upper bowl of the stadium. A tireless worker, few understood just how much time he put in to get the results that typically appeared to come so easily. Five starts into the young season, the results just hadn't been there.

"You're talking about a guy who many had pegged as a Cy Young candidate and here we are in May, and honestly, how many more chances is he going to get to figure it out at the big league level?"

Ouch. That was harsh.

"Are you suggesting that the Phillies send him down to get on track at Triple-A? That might be a little extreme. He's a star in the making, he just needs a little time." *Thank you*, Tanner thought.

"That's what I'm suggesting – you said it yourself that he's been their biggest disappointment this –"

"His *performance* has been disappointing, absolutely. But it's early and I think he's earned the opportunity to get himself right at this level." Tanner fumbled for the remote, but he couldn't pull his eyes away. Watching media coverage of his career was always a surreal experience. It didn't affect him much when they sang his praises, but watching people debate his value without context for how hard he was working to turn his season around took some getting used to.

"I know, I know – he's had a nice career." *Oh, great. Now they're going to marginalize my past accomplishments*, he thought. "But I see a guy with a 0-4 record and an 8.28 ERA. The strikeouts aren't there either. He's taking a major step backward and he just doesn't have –"

The TV went black and Tanner took a deep breath. He couldn't take much more. Not now, not when he was just starting to feel like himself again.

No wins, four losses, and an 8.28 ERA. As much as his coaches told him to forget about his earlier starts, as often as they reminded him that it was still early, it gnawed at him. He felt as though he had turned a corner in his previous start, his first six-inning outing of the season, and he knew that watching so-called experts lay into him did him no favors. Still, it was hard to look away and the stats were hard to ignore.

"I thought I told you not to watch that crap." Tanner turned to find his pitching coach leaning in the doorway. There was no telling how long he had been watching his ace torment himself. Clearly, however, he had seen plenty.

"I know, I know. I just can't help myself." Tanner stood and pressed his practice uniform across his chest. If Arroyo was here, that meant the rest of the pitching staff wouldn't be too far behind. No sense letting the rest of the guys see their staff leader so vulnerable.

"That's just it, you're not helping yourself." Pedro Arroyo put his hands on the young man's shoulders and looked him straight in the eyes. "What do those morons know? Think they can tell the difference between a slider and a heavy curve? Hell, think they've even seen you pitch this season? I'll tell you what I think: they couldn't lace your cleats and they're not worth your time."

"I try not to put too much stock in it, but the numbers are hard to look at."

"To hell with the numbers, son. Don't look at 'em. I've seen every pitch you've thrown this season. It's coming." Arroyo patted Tanner on the side of the head like a father might do to his son. He had that way about him – tough, but fair; stern, but caring. Arroyo was one in a million if you asked any of the pitchers on his staff, and to a man, they did their best to put their own neurosis aside and take his advice. Despite closing out April with the worst pitching line of his career, Tanner was committed to following the old man's instruction. After all, nothing else seemed to work.

"Thanks for talking this stuff through with me. Appreciate you pulling me out of my funk." Tanner meant it. He needed a kick in the ass every now and then.

"Today is the first day of a new month and the slate is clean. If you put up some zeros tomorrow, that ERA you're so concerned about will be a distant memory."

The sound of cleats echoed in the corridor that led to the quiet clubhouse, announcing the arrival of the rest of the team's arms. Until tomorrow, Tanner would find himself swept up in the whirlwind of sound. He patted Arroyo on the shoulder and shifted to his locker to collect his glove and a resistance band. After a bit of stretching, he would spend a few minutes chatting his teammates on the cavernous outfield lawn at Coors Field, home of the Colorado Rockies, and signing autographs for anyone donning a red cap along the foul line.

It would be a good night, he imagined. Tomorrow, when he stepped atop the pitching mound with a fresh outlook on his season, would be even better.

9

Draft Preparations

It would be quaint to say that big league front offices have evolved due to the increased use of analytics and widespread acceptance of data as a tool for scouting, performance enhancement, and roster construction. That only scratches the surface of the extent to which the game has changed during the past decade. Certainly, there has been change and it has been dramatic. All 30 Major League ball clubs utilize advanced analytics to some degree, some in ways so significant that its adoption redefined how the team's scouting and player development operations functioned. The Pittsburgh Pirates, for example, famously built their teams of the 2010s with a focus on unorthodox and frequent (by conventional standards) fielding shifts and acquired several pitchers who thrived in front of a sound infield defense – namely, pitch-to-contact, ground ball types. In the American League, the Oakland Athletics' approach in the early 2000s led to the rise of "Moneyball," which author Michael Lewis turned into a book and then others transformed into a movie. During recent years, the subtle, effective skill of pitch framing at the catcher position has become just as hot a topic in the front office as home runs and batting average, which had been staples of performance evaluation in decades past. So yes, the art of determining both a ballplayer's value and potential differs greatly today in comparison to past eras. There are more Ivy League-educated economists and Google-trained data scientists in front offices today than ever before. The Phillies, however, were late to the party.

Few would argue that the team's current success could be attributed to anything other than its reimagined player development and scouting philosophies implemented under General Manager Mark Johnson. During a few short years, Johnson educated his lieutenants and the broader organization in a new way of thinking about its chief currency: the players on the active roster and at every level of the farm system. His approach centered on a mindset that blended traditional scouting with science and data. As one of the last teams to employ a data analyst and one of the last to stubbornly continue to proclaim itself an ambassador for traditional scouting, Johnson knew when he signed on in Philadelphia that he had his work cut out for him. In short order, the Phillies' front office became a pipeline to the best and brightest minds from Silicon Valley and the top talent graduating from the nation's most highly ranked engineering programs. The beauty of what Johnson had accomplished, however, was in forcing Philadelphia into the future without alienating its past. The team still employed a deep bench of respected scouts and, if anything, Johnson hired more. He never wanted the team to miss out on a future star in the Amateur Draft simply because no one had seen the kid play. Even amid the influx of fresh-faced college graduates with radical ideas, Johnson believed in the value of watching players play the game, and he formulated his opinions of talent based on a combination of insights shared by both departments. And so, it was this school of thought that led to the Phillies replenishing their barren farm system and resurrecting the big league franchise from the depths of the National League. "Consider everything" was his mantra.

Of course, the transformation was not without headaches. Growing pains are unavoidable when you endeavor to rewrite the rules of scouting and player analysis. Add to the mix a few larger-than-life egos and the stubbornness that comes with a room full of confident and experienced baseball lifers, and what you're left with is quite a combustible cocktail. There were a few hurt feelings along the way; a few raised voices, and a few departmental departures that coincided with the deployment of data scientists into Johnson's operation. The turmoil that first accompanied Johnson's front office mindset shift, however, wasn't unique to Philadelphia. Rather, traditional scouting philosophies and new age analytics have never blended without their share of friction. Now, a few years later, the benefits of Johnson's approach had crystallized and the new structure that brought data and scouting insights to the table left little cause for animosity. Heated debate rages on in any meeting that brings scouts and analysts together, but debate is healthy; debate leads to better decisions. Better decisions create a more competitive ball club. And in the end, that's the goal of every general manager.

The June Amateur Draft was still a month away, but there never was a true start or end date for preparations. To be sure, the role of general manager is a 24/7/365 kind of job. But then again, short of an occasional fishing trip and the chance to spend a little extra time with family, there wasn't much else Johnson would rather do with his time. That was true of many of his direct reports as well. Some of whom sat around a conference table on this day, a rainy morning in May.

"Alex, what do you have on Wilcox?" The player in question was a third baseman named Gregory Wilcox, completing his final season at Vanderbilt. The discussion centered on potential selections that might still be on the board when the Phillies made their first-round selection at number nine.

"Line drive hitter, can hit it to all fields. Defense grades out above-average, and I have no doubt that we can leave him at third and he'll thrive." Alex was Alex Corino, head of baseball research and analytics. "From my perspective, the numbers say he's a safe pick at nine. I think Coop was happy with him too, right?"

"I'd be thrilled with Wilcox at nine, absolutely." Marcus Cooper represented the most senior voice of the Phillies traditional scouts, the old-school perspective that Johnson liked to blend with Corino's new school data. Cooper never viewed Corino as a threat even as some scouts within the organization became rankled by the team's increased reliance on data analysts. If the goal was to find the best players, he had been known to say, why not approach scouting from every possible angle? He believed in the players he brought forward and took pride in the fact that Corino's data often validated his recommendations. Cooper's acceptance of new thinking, appreciated by his GM, had a trickle-down effect that, over time, created an open-minded attitude up and down the scouting organization. "The kid has power and from what I saw at Vandy, quick reflexes at the hot corner that will absolutely play up at this level. He's gonna be a player and I see him moving through the system quickly."

"What about Riley? His upside is sky-high." Johnson played the role of moderator in this pre-Draft meeting. He served up names and let his team deliberate. Sometimes there was agreement, like with Wilcox, other times debate. The final call was his and his alone, but he didn't often interject with his own opinions at these early stages of the process. The men and women around the table presented their cases based on months of analysis and study.

Johnson kept his own leanings to himself until the time came to make a decision.

"He could be an ace if he realizes his immense potential." A new voice chimed in with perspective on a lanky left-handed starting pitcher named Michael Riley. It belonged to Hannah Channing, one of Cooper's scouts. "High school kids are always a roll of the dice, but he has a plus-plus curve, a nasty four-seamer, good changeup, and a clean bill of health. He has the tools."

"Can he harness them consistently? That's the big question," Cooper interjected. "He's smooth to the plate, but his arm slot gets out of whack sometimes. Enough to spook me at nine."

"Some nights, I see a baby Kershaw out there." That Channing conjured the name of one of the game's greats, Clayton Kershaw, was all her colleagues needed to hear to understand how she felt about Riley's potential. "But you're right, he gets himself off-kilter from time to time. I'd imagine it isn't anything that can't be corrected; it's a tough call with the first pick."

Channing had been an anomaly when she first wrapped her fingers around a radar gun and sat on a set of dusty bleachers with a gaggle of men twice her age. Simply put, in a world filled with men wearing khakis and polos, she was one-of-a-kind: quite often, the only female scout in attendance. Slowly – ever so slowly – baseball's scouting landscape has changed. Still in the minority, more women than ever before now hold positions as associate and area scouts, and a few have ascended toward the top of the food chain in big league front offices. Inside the Phillies' scouting organization, Channing had built a solid body of work and was a trusted voice in any conversation about amateur ballplayers. One-of-a-kind once again, but only because she was one of Cooper's finest scouts.

"It's so hard to project a high school hurler." Johnson pulled his hands behind his head and looked toward the whiteboard, which held the names of dozens of young players on pliable, rectangular magnets stacked in columns like children's building blocks. One of those magnets would be plucked from the board in a few weeks' time as the Phillies' first round pick. "But if you hit on one, boy, it could be special."

"I like him," Channing continued. "I see the potential for him to be a star, though he's a long way off and I don't know if I'd pick him over a guy at another position that might be closer to contributing."

"No chance he'll fall to us in the second?" The Amateur Draft always brought a few welcome surprises, and Johnson wondered if Riley might be one of them. "Maybe other teams are having this same conversation. Maybe they'll be scared off?"

"Stranger things have happened, but I don't see it." Corino was confident Riley would be a top-15 pick based on what the numbers had shown. "When he's on, he's dominant. And if anyone else has visions of Kershaw when Riley pitches…"

"He'll be long gone." Cooper finished Corino's thought. "The trick is finding that second rounder that'll help ease the blow if we pass on Riley. I like DeLeon, the kid from Arizona."

"Great stuff, lower ceiling than Riley, but a higher floor." Channing had seen Ricky DeLeon several times during the past year, but such was the life of the scout. Like her peers, she would commit the better part of a year patrolling a territory, watching so many ball games that they started to blend, searching for that diamond in the rough. Often, she watched and recommended players who would sign with other teams. However, every now and then the Phillies selected one of her recommendations and it remained her greatest professional joy to watch her picks blossom from minor league dreamers into bona fide big leaguers. "He has a tremendous physique, heavy fastball with movement. He could be a late first rounder, but if we're lucky, we might be able to grab him in the second."

"I'd agree with that," Corino affirmed. "He just pounds the zone more consistently than any high school kid I've seen in quite some time. He fits here, though like any high school kid it'll take a while. I'd say he's further along than most, however."

Johnson glanced at his watch and clapped his hands, signifying the end of another grueling prep session. They had deliberated for almost three hours and though much work remained, Johnson and his team had made significant headway with about a month to go before the draft. For weeks, they compared notes, updated reports with fresh data and scouting insights, and moved names around on the whiteboard. More and more, a college infielder was emerging as priority one: Gregory Wilcox. Would he be on the board when the Phillies picked at number nine? It was impossible to know for sure. In earlier sessions, they had settled on a few alternatives – a catcher from South Florida, a high school shortstop that reminded many of franchise icon Jimmy Rollins, and another college pitcher. Months of scouting, thousands of miles logged, thousands of hours at the computer, and it would all come to a head in four weeks. And for all their efforts, there was no way of knowing whether it was even a modestly successful draft for several years down the road. But that's the game – their game – and they loved it.

"Good work, people. Same time tomorrow." His team filed out of the conference room one by one, leaving the general manager alone to study the names on the board once more. Listed on that board was at least one ballplayer, maybe more, who he hoped could be part of the future in Philadelphia. When that future would arrive, if it arrived at all, was anyone's guess. Amateur ballplayers might play well enough in the high school or college ranks to earn their shot. What happened after that, what they did with the opportunity, was largely up to them. A blend of hard work, good coaching, and a whole lot of luck. That part, too, the human element that led to both triumph and failure, made the success stories mean so much more.

10

On the Beat

The commercial flights don't get any easier.

Tom Flanagan, on the Phillies beat for the past decade at the *Philadelphia Inquirer*, recalled a time when criss-crossing the U.S. was exciting. A new city to explore every few days, a new ballpark to cross off his list. These days, road trips aren't met with the same enthusiasm.

"Three-hour delay. Three fucking hours on the tarmac at Philly International," Flanagan shouted to a peer arriving at a nearby gate in Denver. Rebecca Stoyanos covered the Phillies for a competing news site, but press box friendships know no boundaries. When you're a hard-working scribe living out of a suitcase and facing daily deadlines on a daily basis, the camaraderie between writers can sometimes be the only thing that keeps you going on the baseball grind, equal parts tedium and panic. "I hate these damn airports."

"Wearing down already, Tom? We've got a long way to go." Stoyanos fell in alongside him and the two quickened their pace through the airport. Years of practice had prepared both for navigating flight delays and unforeseen travel hiccups. A three-hour delay, while a nuisance, still left plenty of time to get to the ballpark before the action started. "Denver is always full of surprises. I should have been here a couple of hours ago too."

"Share a cab?"

"That'll work." Flanagan had known Stoyanos for most of his decade on the beat. While he had remained with the *Inquirer* for much of his adult life, working first on the metro desk before moving to sports, where he covered hockey and then baseball, she had hopped around from one media property to the next. While the employer changed every couple of years, the Phillies remained her focus since leaving Villanova for the working world. In 12 years, she had seen a World Champion and a number one draft pick – the prizes for Major League Baseball's best team and its worst, respectively. She watched future Hall of Famers arrive to much fanfare and depart quietly, replaced by a collection of anonymous replacement-level minor leaguers. And, in recent times, she had seen the cycle begin anew with the team's return to contention. This time, however, the pieces falling into place were mostly of the homegrown variety, which stood in stark contrast to the blend of high-priced free agent splashes from year's past. This year's team reminded her of the early days just before the Phillies' 2008 World title-winning squad: creeping closer to contention even if they weren't quite ready to boat race the league.

"How's that story on Alvarez coming? He seems to be adapting well to the game." Jose Alvarez, the Phillies most exciting offseason mystery, was on everyone's mind in South Philly. Blessed with natural ability and a short swing, the Cuban import slid into the starting lineup on Opening Day and hadn't looked back. A natural in the field and at the plate, he entered his second month of big league ball hitting .361, and ranked atop the league's stolen base charts with 14 swipes without being caught. The power, prodigious in Cuba's professional baseball leagues, was the last of his abilities to manifest. Homerless through the team's first 27 games, the front office brass didn't much care if he ever left the yard if he kept turning singles into doubles and doubles into triples with his video game speed.

"He's a delight. An absolute delight." Stoyanos couldn't contain her enthusiasm for her subject. "Once his English improves, you watch – the league is going to fall in love with this guy."

"That's got to be the hardest thing in the world, coming to a new league in a new country and only being able to express a fraction of who you are." Times had changed, of course, for Cuban baseball players making the jump to big league life in America. No longer were they forced to seek out middle-of-the-night passage with unsavory traffickers or island-hop their way toward U.S. shores, trying to stay one step ahead of capture. The baseball archives are riddled with horror stories of the harrowing flight of the Cuban ballplayer. Fathers separated from children, sons who may never see their mothers again. The world was changing, but Alvarez still faced some of the same challenges that come with starting over in a strange new place.

"He's fun to watch – lightning-quick bat speed. Hard to get anything by him," Stoyanos continued. "It'll be fascinating theater to see what kinds of adjustments he makes when the league gets a book on him. For now, it's just good fun."

"I should say so." Flanagan's mind was already scattering in a dozen directions while he listened to Stoyanos. A decade ago, beat reporters only needed to worry about filing their game report and perhaps a supporting piece or two before wrapping up a few minutes past midnight each day. Now, thanks to the proliferation of social networks and the always-on expectations of the Phillies' fan base, Flanagan and the rest of the beats sprayed content in

every direction all game long. It wasn't enough to manu-
facture a perfect lede, craft a handful of well-constructed
paragraphs, and dress it all up at the end of the night with
a few primo quotes. Instead, the role of the beat reporter
had evolved into something different. He or she served as
the unbiased eyes and ears of the fan, reporting the action
from first pitch to final out, sharing the story of both the
pivotal moments and the mundane. For Flanagan, only
after hours of constant content creation across a host of
social channels and the *Inquirer*'s Phillies blog could he
pause to file stories for the newspaper's print edition.
Would anyone even read his articles in the newspaper the
next morning? In the 24/7 reality of sports reporting, even
the best writing becomes stale in the blink of an eye.

The taxi eased to a stop in front of Coors Field, quiet
but for an occasional autograph hunter or family mulling
over options at the ticket window. Coors Field, now standing for a quarter century, had been designed by architects
who followed the model made popular by the Baltimore
Orioles with the opening of Oriole Park at Camden Yards.
Nestled in the heart of Denver's picturesque downtown
district, the stadium was a pleasant blend of old and new:
new in that it was built toward the end of the twentieth
century, but it also possessed enough of the old-time
charm to carry a hint of nostalgia. Once inside, all the
familiar trappings and technological advancements made
themselves known in spite of the classic, curved atrium at
the main gate, which offered the slightest notion of long
since-demolished hardball cathedrals like Shibe Park,
Ebbets Field, and many others from days gone by.

"I like coming here," Flanagan said as the two reporters entered the main gate. "Denver is a fun little city. I like
how they jammed this stadium right in here amid the
shops and restaurants – not that I ever have much time for
shops and restaurants while we're here, of course."

"I'd live here," Stoyanos said. "Put me on the Rockies' beat, I'm ready to explore this place."

"Even in the winter? Picture Philly in February, only colder and with more snow." Flanagan shuddered at the thought. If his job provided any comfort these days, it was that amid the gauntlet of air travel, he would feel the heat of South Florida in summertime at least a few times each year.

"Bring it on!" They laughed and hastened their pace up the ramp toward the press box and dining hall. While the writers don't often enjoy the perks afforded to their better-compensated interview subjects, big league teams try their best to keep their scribes well-fed.

"Hey, Tom. Becca." Phillies manager John McGown, in full uniform, passed them in the hall leading to the press box. "What's the good word?"

"Holding it together, John." Flanagan and McGown exchanged handshakes and the manager patted Stoyanos on the shoulder. "Not quite as well as you, it seems. 17-10, not a bad start. That's got to feel good."

"We're finding a groove. Swinging the bats well." McGown turned to Stoyanos and his eyes lit up as if he had just recalled a distant memory. "How's the Alvarez piece? Is Don getting you what you need?"

"He's my new best friend," she replied, referring to Don Hollingsworth, the team's Media Relations Director. "He's been great. I was just telling Tom, you've got a good kid on your hands with Jose."

"We like him." McGown smiled and bid the writers farewell. They'd meet again in a few hours following the game. Visiting teams aren't afforded the same regal press conference setup that follows home games, but McGown would field questions from a dozen or so writers, recorders in hand, seated in a cramped side office off the visiting locker room. He wasn't always enthusiastic – that depended on the outcome of the game – but McGown offered his time whether he wanted to or not. His late-night reunions with the press, however, were less loathsome after a win.

"Tom, you taking the over on runs scored?" Flanagan shook his head and continued typing his response to a fan's question on Twitter. The question, anxiety about the team's ace, had become a recurring theme in his news feed and one he tried to quell whenever it popped up. No sense panicking about Aaron Tanner after a handful of bad starts in the season's first month. Flanagan had seen enough ups and downs in 10 years on the beat to know that the kid was good enough to turn his season around. He'd bet on it if he was a betting man. He'd also take the under.

"This ballpark gets a bad rap," he said in reply to Mark Dorfman, a writer from a Delaware County paper. "What is it, 5-4 in the sixth? I'd take the under."

"That's a lot of confidence in those bullpen arms." Dorfman loved to talk wagers, though it was all in good fun.

"I can't speak for the Rockies' pen, but Arroyo's got Philly pitching well." Flanagan always believed that the bullpen life was a flimsy one. Year to year, aside from a few lights-out closers, you never quite know what to expect. For the most part, the Phillies hadn't experienced too many missteps in the late innings. "Peterson has been a revelation."

"Talk about a good story. Looks like they struck gold with that guy." Dorfman, perhaps more than most, appreciated the redemption story unfolding from the arm of the Phillies' lefty specialist, Bennett Peterson. The first to report on his signing just before Spring Training, he wrote a series of feature pieces on the man's journey from the edge of obscurity to early season sensation. After the season's first month, he had been nearly unhittable and had not been scored upon in 11 innings. Even more impressive, he had yet to allow a walk, his fatal flaw in past seasons. Each spring, Dorfman's editor allowed him to choose one player to track closely and this season, much like the team's front office, choosing Peterson had proven to be a stroke of brilliance. On this night, Peterson would enter the game in the seventh inning, tasked with protecting a two-run lead with two runners on base and a couple tough lefties at the plate. Eight pitches and two strikeouts later, he was back in the dugout and the team was well on its way to another victory, barring a late-game meltdown. In this ballpark, however, where the ball flew like a rocket through the thin, mile-high air, no lead was safe.

"That was a big spot," Stoyanos announced to her peers from the second row of the press box. "Nasty stuff."

"You said it." As was customary, especially late in a game with fast-approaching deadlines looming, a phantom response emerged from the pool of reporters, all with fingers tapping away at keyboards, eyes alternating between the action on the field and the words pouring from their fingertips onto their computer screens. Stoyanos didn't know the source of the reply, but it didn't matter. A quick acknowledgment, and it was back to work.

Tonight, the first night in a new city, the first of the team's longest road trip of the young season, there would be no cause for anxiety. No reason for a couple dozen reporters to rip up their game reports and start over. The Phillies' bullpen held its lead and the offense tacked on a couple more runs to pull away. From every corner of the press box, reporters published their first articles just as the Phillies' closer and catcher met for a handshake between home plate and the mound after the final pitch of the night. By 10:30 p.m., the traveling beat writers had crowded around McGown's desk for a few choice quotes and within the next 45 minutes, each had circulated through the visitor's clubhouse for sound bites from the heroes of the night. Flanagan and his peers spent a couple minutes with big first baseman Barrett Taylor, who continued his hot hitting by knocking in a couple runs with a big fifth inning double. They would shuffle along to Peterson, the quiet giant, who had extended his mastery of opposing lefties. And finally, Richie LeGrande, the team's beleaguered left fielder, who amid an otherwise frustrating campaign, started the scoring with a second inning two-run homer. Smiles all around for the visitors, and some blaring old-school hip-hop for good measure – chosen by everyone's favorite clubhouse leader, Marcel Valentín. Moments before midnight, the men and women on the Phillies beat had refreshed game reports, uploaded each story to various web sites and social platforms, and submitted their final articles for the morning print run. It was May 1, the Phillies were winning, and spirits were at an all-time high. Everyone in road grays on a crisp Colorado night, along with the dedicated beat writers on the hunt for good stories, hoped the good times would keep rolling as spring turned to summer, summer to fall.

11

Draft Day

Somewhere in the distance, children squealed while posing for photos with two oversized mice. Rides modeled after famous movie franchises sent children and their families on a mild adrenaline rush in between the drudgery of lengthy lines. Somewhere in the distance, the wonder of Walt Disney World entertained and delighted. Not here, however. Representatives from every Major League Front Office descended upon this magical little city in Central Florida, but its rides, characters, and performances were of little consequence to the sport's top executives. Draft day has that kind of distracting effect on the architects of the game's future.

A rectangular, glass conference room buzzed with energy and a cacophony of noise despite only fits and starts of conversation by its inhabitants. Television broadcasts from the league's official network filled the room with analysis and debate. Video footage of the top high school and college athletes played on a loop across a dozen computer screens. Meanwhile, in every palm and pocket, still more connected devices remained alight with exhaustive analysis and background information about the young men who might, in a matter of moments, be on the path toward stardom in Philadelphia.

To General Manager Mark Johnson, Draft Day delivered both the excitement of Christmas morning and the anxiety of a job interview rolled into one. Equal parts excitement and nervousness. Equal parts joy and fear. Despite the emotional rollercoaster, the Amateur Draft was by far his favorite event of the year.

"How we looking at six? Twins take an outfielder here, no?" Eyes trained on the big screen, he shouted to everyone at once and to no one in particular. On the screen and stationed in the league's broadcast studio, Jack Forrest, a retired outfielder and fan favorite, sat at a long table with other team representatives from across the league. He was waiting for a call from Johnson that would reveal the Phillies' pick, but for now, he sat alongside fellow alumni from other teams with hands clasped, waiting for the Minnesota Twins to pluck a name off the board. This was something new for Major League Baseball. While other sports leagues turned their own annual drafts into massive, public spectacles, baseball only recently transformed its Amateur Draft into must-see TV.

"That would be logical," Hannah Channing, one of the Phillies' lead scouts, spoke up first. "All signs point to Pointer, funny enough."

Representatives from the Phillies' front office and scouting departments, 14 in all, held their collective breath as Johnson raised a hand to call for silence. The pick was in. The Twins' rep spent a moment on the phone, placed it back on its cradle, and leaned toward the microphone just in front of him.

"The Minnesota Twins select Sabastiano Prep outfielder Daniel Pointer with the sixth pick in the draft." The television broadcast switched to a living room somewhere in Central Iowa where a high school outfielder celebrated with a gaggle of friends and family members. Daniel Pointer was headed for a major payday as the league's sixth overall draft selection. The Phillies, zeroing in on other players, were equally excited for the young man, though for different reasons. Tight applause and deep exhales sounded throughout the conference room as one more threat to the team's plans fell off the board. As their selection drew closer, the Phillies inched toward making a third baseman from Vanderbilt the ninth pick in the draft.

"Two more picks," Johnson said through a deep breath. "If Wilcox is there at nine I'm going to lose my shit." Gregory Wilcox possessed skills that were easy to dream on. As a polished 21-year-old with above-average defensive ability and a sky-high ceiling at the plate, Johnson, his data scientists, and scouts all agreed that Wilcox could be a fixture at the hot corner for many years to come. "Riley is still there too, but we've got to go with the bat this year. I feel strongly about that," he continued.

Johnson paced the room. Like a tiger in a cage, he walked back and forth, deep in thought but also tuned into the conversations around him. The Diamondbacks picked next and based on the depth of their minor league system, Johnson worried that Arizona's most glaring needs called for a corner infielder who could be fast-tracked to the big leagues. After Arizona came Oakland, another franchise with a gaping hole at third and every reason to pick a guy like Wilcox. But then, maybe Arizona would go for Lou Portman, the high school second baseman who was still sitting there at seven, even though he had been tipped to go as early as third overall. Could the Diamondbacks pass on a premier middle infield talent? And after Arizona, perhaps the A's would become enamored with the big arm of right-handed starter Michael Frandsen. Tantalizing talent in every direction and, if Johnson had his way, just enough to blind his rivals from the Phillies' top target.

A hush fell over the room as the Diamondbacks' representative reached for the phone to receive the team's pick at seven.

"Here it is, people. It's Wilcox or Portman." Johnson stopped pacing and stared daggers at the television as if he could telepathically will the Diamondbacks' pick to be Portman through the TV screen.

"The Arizona Diamondbacks select Lou Portman, second baseman, East Looma High School, with the seventh selection of the draft."

The room exploded once again with applause. This time with a bit more urgency than before. The Phillies were one pick away from setting their course and, potentially, shaping the future of their organization. Of course, the Amateur Draft offered little in the way of guarantees. Each year, the first round delivered nearly as many busts as big leaguers and arguably more busts than superstars. The Phillies were banking on Gregory Wilcox to buck those odds.

Johnson understood that a team's first selection, while a culmination of months of deliberation about the player upon whom they would bestow the honor, was just the beginning. Truly, success in the draft wouldn't be known for several years and even then, would only be judged, for better or worse, on the outcome of the team's selections long after the celebrated first rounder. In fact, the team could whiff on its first pick and still look back on its effort with pride if the next several rounds yielded Major League talent. Still, Johnson wanted Wilcox at number nine and only the Oakland Athletics stood in the way. It mattered little that his staff had pulled together a list of 30 possible first round picks – a list that still held many available names. Anything short of Wilcox would be disappointing to the front office chief.

"Mark, depending on where the A's go here, we should also consider Julio Tavares out of Highland Park." Alex Corino, Johnson's trusted data analyst, handed his GM a stack of papers. Some featured colorful spray charts of the young catcher's hitting tendencies while others featured charts upon charts of numbers that, when deciphered, pointed to a player's true value as a batter, fielder, and baserunner. "His pitch framing is well above average for his age and the bat is far more mature than most at the position – even compared to the college guys."

"Coop, remind me of your take on Tavares," Johnson shouted across the room to Marcus Cooper, the team's scouting director. That Johnson sought Cooper's input on the high school catcher was no slight to Corino, and the team's lead analyst took no offense. Johnson had rebuilt a barren Phillies farm system by taking in perspectives and analysis from all all his top confidants and he wasn't about to stop now.

"Good kid. Strong. He has a quick bat and he'll grow into the position." Glasses resting on the tip of his nose, Cooper sat at a long conference table and continued to sift through notes that wouldn't become relevant for another couple of rounds. While his general manager fixated on the team's first pick, Cooper was already preparing for the next several decisions that awaited. "Very mature abilities for a high school senior, though he's a little wild behind the dish. Coachable, though."

"You like him over Riley here?" Johnson had fallen hard for the talented pitcher with electric stuff, but like many around the league, his staff had become wary of his recent inconsistency. He remained, arguably, the pitcher with the highest ceiling in the draft. Still, he was no sure thing.

"I do." Channing spoke first. "The way this is playing out, I think Riley may fall to the second round – he might still be on the board for us there."

"Best available at nine? Assuming Wilcox is gone?" There was movement among the A's Draft Day representatives on the big screen, which caught Johnson's attention. It was almost time.

"After Wilcox? Probably Miller, the center fielder from UCLA." Corino poured over his notes as he spoke, quickly ripping a few sheets on Miller from his notebook and handing them to Johnson for further consideration. Miller, a speedy all-world defender, was on the Phillies' radar somewhere behind Wilcox and Tavares, possibly Riley too, in terms of prioritization. "Bat's a little suspect today, but he's a gifted athlete and has the talent to be a star."

Johnson studied the notes on Miller before turning back to the screen. The A's representative reached for the phone and the Phillies' brass quieted and held their collective breath. The call had come in.

"With the eighth pick, the Oakland Athletics select Michael Frandsen, starting pitcher, Mississippi State."

"It's Wilcox! Make the call – I don't need to wait on this one." Johnson hugged Corino and offered congratulations to the rest of his staff while Cooper, Channing, and the rest of the team did the same in the team's makeshift war room outside of Walt Disney World. The A's representative hardly finished reporting Oakland's selection before the phone rang and Forrest received news of the Phillies selection. In a few short moments, the Phillies had made Gregory Wilcox, a polished third baseman from Vanderbilt, their first-round pick and then turned their attention to the rounds that followed. He was their top priority, though not their only priority. Truly, the Amateur Draft left little time for celebration.

———

Gregory Wilcox squeezed his mother's hand in the family's living room while extended family and dozens of friends crowded together in front of the television. The Phillies had given him their assurance that he wouldn't fall any further than the draft's ninth overall pick and he had offered his commitment to signing with the team should they hold up their end of the bargain. For a young ball-player hanging on the precipice, however, nothing ever felt like a stone-cold lock. Not when history has shown can't-miss prospects falling to later rounds, unknowns soaring to the top of the pile, and more than a thousand high school and college ballplayers waited on pins and needles for their names to be called.

"This has to be it, baby. It's Oakland or Philadelphia, not a doubt in my mind." Sharon Wilcox clutched her son's hand with all her might and tried to put his mind at ease as the family approached the moment they hoped would set in motion the next phase of the young man's life. "They both liked you, Greg, but it sure felt like you were at the top of the list for Philadelphia – don't you think?"

"It's so hard to say, mom." Wilcox's calm response betrayed the nerves he felt as the Athletics' draft day representative hung up the phone and reached for the microphone. Based on his interactions with the Athletics' front office, he wasn't so sure his path led to Oakland. Still, anything was possible. "Things change quickly. I'll be happy anywhere."

"I know you will, baby. And you'll do well anywhere too."

"Here it comes…" A voice from the doorway that led into the living room from the kitchen caused a quiet to fall over the room. A cousin, perhaps. Maybe one of his teammates. Wilcox didn't dare look away from the screen that would inform him of his destiny at any moment.

"With the eighth pick, the Oakland Athletics select Michael Frandsen, starting pitcher, Mississippi State."

The Athletics announced their pick and it wasn't a popular choice in the Wilcox household. To his credit, Wilcox maintained composure while friends patted him on the shoulder in case he needed consoling. He didn't.

"Okay, well it's Philly then." Another voice came from behind as Wilcox's mother continued to clutch her son's hand – a grasp that grew tighter as the picks came in. It was Philly. It had to be. "Look! Forrest is reaching for the phone already! They're making their pick!"

This was a surprising development even if the team had been open about their intentions. Wilcox cracked a smile; in a matter of seconds, his entire life was about to change. Philadelphia didn't need to wait to make their pick – their guy was on the board and it was time to pull him down.

"The Philadelphia Phillies select Gregory Wilcox, third baseman, Vanderbilt University, with the ninth pick in the draft."

Now, he could celebrate. Now, he could release the emotions he held in check all evening. Wilcox hardly made it to his feet before he was mobbed by loved ones and teammates.

"We did it!" He shouted above the uproarious applause, cheers, and laughter. Wilcox was the only person in the room that had been, or would be, selected in the draft. His support system ran so deep, however, that they all felt as though they had a stake in his good fortune. No one felt more fortunate for those around him than the man who would soon enter the Phillies minor league system. "It'll be a long road ahead. Thank you – all of you – for sharing in this with me. I love you guys!"

How anyone heard the phone ringing is a mystery. On the other end of the line, speaking to the Phillies' third baseman of the future, was Wilcox's agent, Grant Wilson. The conversation was brief, and interrupted by alternating chants of "LET'S GO, PHILLY!" and "WIL-COX! WIL-COX!" However, the two men said all that needed to be said. Once he signed, Wilson said, the Phillies planned to put Wilcox on the fast-track. Most draft picks start out in rookie ball, but Wilcox was on another level. As a polished college player, he would begin his pro journey another rung up the ladder with the team's short-season affiliate in Williamsport, Penn.

"From there, the sky's the limit," Wilson said.

In Williamsport, in Philadelphia, wherever. The path for Gregory Wilcox changed for good on a warm night in June. As he finished up his call and returned to the party, he knew one thing for certain: the hard work was just beginning, and he couldn't wait to get started.

12

UCL

The throbbing sensation wasn't new, but whether it was a symptom of fear or disbelief, he had managed to keep it to himself for going on two months. Ignoring a problem seldom resolves underlying issues, of course. Somewhere buried beneath the skin, nestled inside Daniel Baker's right elbow, a problem was metastasizing and becoming unbearable.

It was the dip in velocity that first caught the attention of the Phillies' managerial and training staffs. With the benefit of hindsight, Baker's performance, ever at the mercy of the usual ups and downs of the big league season though seldom a cause for concern, had offered clues that something wasn't quite right. Of course, pitchers sometimes pitch poorly – it's the nature of the game. So, when a reliable veteran starter with a proven track record struggles through the first third of the season, you give him the benefit of the doubt and let him work through it. Alarm bells start to ring, however, when that player is a 36-year-old power pitcher who experiences a sudden and dramatic drop in fastball velocity.

"How long have you been experiencing discomfort?" Team doctor Patrick Sheridan spoke in a measured, deliberate tone. No one wanted to state the obvious, but it was clear that Baker, Sheridan, and Phillies manager John McGown, arms crossed and still as a statue, knew where this conversation was headed. Elbow discomfort, particularly among pitchers, breeds panic. All too often, the cause of pain is a tear in the ulnar collateral ligament (UCL), which leads to a procedure known as Tommy John surgery. Pitchers bounce back from tweaked hamstrings and oblique strains. Tommy John surgery? The road back to a big league mound is long and hard.

"I'd say it hasn't felt quite right since late March. I had a couple good outings at the beginning of Spring Training and then I just kind of lost the feel for it."

"I wish you would have told us about it earlier, Dan." McGown put a hand on Baker's shoulder in an expression of empathy. Despite his disappointment, McGown understood that there are shades of gray when it comes to elite athletes performing at the highest level of the game. For a veteran pitcher playing out the last few years of his career, major reconstructive elbow surgery isn't something that's easily confronted. Like an addict, the first step toward recovery is admitting you have a problem. That's easier said than done. "There's no shame in speaking up."

"This game beats you up – you know that, Skipper. I'm always banged up and I just figured this was more of the same." Baker wasn't the first pro athlete to conceal his aches and pains and he wouldn't be the last. And so, he sat on an examination table in early June, in the bowels of the Phillies' ballpark, wondering if he'd ever pitch again.

"It's easy for me to stand here and tell you what you should have done, I know that." McGown understood the conundrum better than most. During his playing days, while not a star, he gained a reputation as a "gamer." In baseball, it's the highest compliment a borderline big leaguer can attain – always game for action, always willing to work hard to stay on the roster, and always willing to play through the bumps and bruises that come with the big league life. McGown never earned a steady role as a player, but he sure as hell played hurt in order to hang onto whatever role he was asked to play. "It's easy for me to say it, but I need to anyway. At the first sign of trouble, raise your hand and speak up. My opinion of you as a ball-player is already formed – you'll never be judged for being honest."

"What happens now? What's next?" Baker had avoided inquiring about what was to come because he already knew the answer and he didn't like it. Still, they couldn't sit in the trainer's office forever.

"I'm going to make an appointment for you with Dr. Ritter. We'll have a better idea of what we're dealing with once he's had a look." Sheridan's plan elicited a groan from Baker, perhaps reflexively. Doctor Ritter. The man had performed more UCL repair surgeries than any in base-ball history and Baker didn't want to be the next. As far as the player's union was concerned, he was both the giver of new life and the harbinger of death. "Look, let's not get ahead of ourselves here. I'm not scheduling you for sur-gery, we're just getting you a proper diagnosis and then we can set a course for the way forward."

"It's a lot to process, Pat. A guy like me doesn't want to spend too much time with a guy like Ritter." The room was cool, but Baker wiped sweat from his forehead and did what he could to calm his racing heart. His words to Sheridan rang true: a pitcher in Baker's position, playing out the final year of his contract and heading into the year-to-year stage of his career, didn't have any interest in making Ritter's acquaintance. As an aging pitcher with a fair amount of mileage on his tires, Baker had been at peace with his future in free agency. He had already come to grips with the reality that the Phillies were moving toward a future without him and he was likely headed to a new zip code during the offseason. Now, he was damaged goods. And if the worst-case scenario materialized and he found himself on the shelf for the next 12-14 months? He'd be lucky if he ever pitched again. The market dries up quickly for a 38-year-old pitcher coming off Tommy John surgery.

"Dan, let's take it one day at a time." McGown was always the voice of reason when his players let their minds wade into dangerous waters. He wasn't a nurturer, but he had his players' best interests at heart and that went a long way. "Don't make yourself crazy worrying about what you can't control or what may or may not be ahead of you. This situation will take care of itself and in the end, however the cards fall, you'll be alright."

"Thanks, Skip," Baker shook McGown's hand and Sheridan helped him to his feet. "If we're done here, I think I'll take a walk. Get some fresh air."

The comfort of summer's late-morning warmth and bright sunshine offered little respite from the chaos that churned in Baker's mind. A baseball player since his earliest memories, he had been a middle-of-the-rotation big league starter for more than a decade and had tallied respectable numbers with four ball clubs during his time at the game's highest level. It had been a good career, a source of pride. After more than a decade, the past four seasons with Philadelphia, was it all over just like that? He wandered the perimeter of the ballpark and memories from his life in baseball fluttered to the fore before dissipating again to the background, each one replaced by another distant memory bubbling to the surface. He thought of his mechanics: the peculiar throwing motion that made him so menacing on the mound and now threatened to steal away the last couple years of his career. Who dreamt up the concept of throwing baseballs overhanded, anyway? The over-the-shoulder release deployed by all pitchers apart from a select few masters of the sidearm or submarine delivery, comes with a great deal of injury risk. It's unorthodox; it goes against the natural movements of the human body. For a ballplayer like Baker, however, few experiences could deliver more satisfaction than rearing back and blowing a batter away with a 98 mile-per-hour heater. He loved every part of the encounter: from the deep breath that accompanied his high leg kick to the rough feel of the laces gliding across his calloused fingertips. Most of all, what stayed in the back of Baker's mind all these years was that glimpse of panic in the batter's eyes when he realizes he can't catch up to that little white seed slipping past his bat. Baker was a pitcher through and through, from the time he was old enough to play organized baseball until the day he dies. To consider that his baseball mortality might be tested after 30 years free of major injury was a tough pill to swallow. *Take it one day at a time*, he thought. That was McGown's advice and he would heed it. He didn't have much choice – either tie himself in knots with worry or push the future, the unknown, from his mind until forced to confront it again. It was mid-June, the Phillies were turning heads in the standings, and Baker would watch from the sidelines until someone, anyone, told him he could play again. He just hoped he'd be given that chance before the Baseball Gods decided that his time in The Show was over.

13

Trade Winds Blowing

The pounding in his head was only muted by the pounding in his chest. Richie LeGrande, a 29-year-old outfielder, stared at the ceiling and wrestled with his poor choices from the night before and anxiety about his future that he just couldn't shake. While baseball players have a long history of balancing on-field excellence with late-night exploits, LeGrande hadn't enjoyed the former in quite some time. And unlike New York Yankees' greats Mickey Mantle and Whitey Ford, men whose after-hours shenanigans were almost as legendary as their Hall of Fame careers, the partying is never quite as legendary when you're drinking by yourself.

It had been that kind of season for LeGrande. Mid-way through June, and with his team flying high, he struggled to bury the negativity to the deepest recesses of his mind. Never the best player on the field, he was sure that this season, he was the worst. LeGrande entered Spring Training as one of several competitors in a hodgepodge of left field options and had separated himself from the pack enough to earn the lion's share of playing time to start the season. Even still, he knew he was only a placeholder until Triple-A prospect Nick Corbin was ready for his call-up. Corbin had struggled to find his footing in the minors, but LeGrande felt the walls closing in anyway. That's what happens when you're heading toward the season's mid-point carrying a .173 average in regular playing time. The brain fog caused by his miserable plate appearances had begun to follow him into the field, and that combination was hard for an impatient fan base to overlook. Boos from the crowd came on quickly and before too long, LeGrande heard that sound resonating from every corner of the ballpark any time he stepped onto the field. Soon, he started hearing it in his head far from the ballpark, too. In the quiet moments at home, in his nightmares. And while the front office wouldn't dare join the chorus, his ineffectiveness was harder and harder for the Phillies' brass to overlook as well.

"What time did you get in last night?" If he didn't know better, LeGrande might have mistaken his roommate, center fielder Preston Saunders, for a concerned parent.

"I don't know." He rolled over and closed his eyes to avoid making eye contact with the man standing in his doorway. "It's all kind of a blur."

"My man, you've got to slow it down. You're not helping yourself out there, Richie." It was strange to hear Saunders, several years his junior, serve as the voice of reason. In any other situation, he might have ignored the guidance of a younger ballplayer, but sharing an apartment with Saunders had given LeGrande perspective. A devout Christian and an equally devoted gym rat, Saunders worked hard to maintain his All-Star status. LeGrande admired his younger teammate, but try as he might, he struggled to adopt the man's discipline. LeGrande couldn't let go of bad habits. He was losing control of his destiny and he knew it.

"I know, Pres. It's all speeding up for me right now." LeGrande sat up and rubbed his pounding temple. "I'm struggling to get myself right."

"Let me get you some water." Saunders turned from the doorway and jogged to the kitchen. "We've got an hour before we have to get to the yard. Go clean yourself up."

Aside from their dramatic off-field differences, Saunders' season was heading in a different direction, too. Among league leaders in several categories, including batting average, runs scored, and doubles, Saunders was well on his way to his fourth All-Star selection and was continuing to evolve into one of the most complete players in the game. That he did it all with the modesty and humulity one might expect of less heralded athletes only added to his growing legacy. He was a dirt dog, a hard-nosed throwback who was as comfortable signing autographs for kids as he was sliding in the muck to avoid a tag. Saunders was wise beyond his years and there were no limits to how far his star could rise.

"I'm heading over early. I can cover for you if you want," Saunders shouted to LeGrande through the bathroom door.

"No need. I'll be there." LeGrande stood still beneath the scalding heat of the shower head. For the first time in a while, he felt human again. "Thanks for the pep talk, Pres. I feel better already."

"Glad to hear it. See you when I see you, brother."

Many rebuilding teams embark on a youth movement and for the Phillies, amid the transition from World Champs to league doormats and back again, the process was no different. Sometimes it works, oftentimes it doesn't. Thus far in their transformation, which had taken several leaps forward during the past couple of years, the Phillies had enjoyed the good fortune of rebuilding with young talent who possessed the right kind of work ethic. If you were inclined to lean on clichés, you might say that they "played the game the right way." All hustle, all effort. Leading by example, Saunders set the tone. A healthy locker room culture can take a solid, unspectacular ball club to great heights. It can also make the outliers, like LeGrande, stand out for all the wrong reasons. Standing in the shower, beneath the pulsing water, he committed to cleaning up his act. For himself, and for teammates like Saunders who depended on him to get his mind right. It wasn't the first time he had made that commitment to himself, but he was growing sick of the empty promises. Something needed to change. He would do all he could to fix what was broken before it was too late – if it wasn't too late already.

———————

"Hey, Richie. Come on in here, would you?" LeGrande had hoped to evade the notice of his teammates and coaches upon arriving at the ballpark, but he couldn't slip past McGown.

"Sure, Mac. What is it?" Tentative, he straightened his back and approached the chair across from his manager in the awkward way someone might when they're trying to be casual. You can't fake casual.

"I just got off the phone with Mark. We made a couple moves this morning." LeGrande sank in his chair, a heavy feeling weighing on his heart. His world was crumbling. A call from the team's GM isn't often a good omen for the guys on the 26-man roster and it's even worse when you're batting .173. "We're bringing in Tyson Jackson from Pittsburgh. He's a bit like Valentín in that he'll give us a professional at-bat from the right side and produce with a couple starts per week."

"Where am I headed?" LeGrande tried to remain calm while his heart beat out of his chest. He had been expecting this moment to come for some time now. Still, it's never an easy conversation. He didn't expect to be heading back to Pittsburgh in exchange for Jackson; that deal might have made sense a couple years ago, but he was a shell of the player he used to be back then. At this point, he simply hoped they'd give him a shot to figure it out with the team's Triple-A ball club in Lehigh Valley.

"Colorado liked what they saw in you a few weeks ago. You had a couple nice at-bats out there." LeGrande exhaled. What a relief. A change of scenery and a second chance in a new organization.

"I did. Think that was the best contact I made all season."

"Well, you made an impression." McGown pushed a few papers aside and leaned toward his former left fielder. "They have a plan for you. You'll get regular at-bats and you won't be under any pressure there."

"Can't help but feel like I blew it with the boys." LeGrande shook his head and looked down at his hands, still shaking from the nerves. Or, maybe the alcohol. "You're bringing in the kind of guy I should have been for this team. I really mucked it up, didn't I?"

"Hindsight is the damnedest thing. Everything is crystal clear now, isn't it?" McGown cracked a smile and folded his arms. "Look, you've got an opportunity ahead of you. Embrace it."

"I will. Thanks, Mac. What's next?"

"Jack has your paperwork," McGown replied, referring to the team's travel secretary Jack Landon. "They're on the road. You'll meet the team in Atlanta."

The two men stood and shook hands before LeGrande returned to his locker to collect a few mementos. *A change of scenery will be good for me*, he thought. Regardless, it was another big league assignment. That would always be better than the alternatives.

"'Bout time you dragged your ass out of that apartment!" LeGrande turned to find that his roommate had joined him in the clubhouse. Drenched with sweat and carrying a couple of bats over his shoulder, it had already been a busy morning for the star center fielder. LeGrande, on the other hand, was heading in another direction.

"I'll be seeing you, Pres." LeGrande reached a hand toward his roommate and brought him in for an embrace.

"Come again?"

"They shipped me out this morning." The words stung as they left his mouth. As hopeful as he was about what awaited him in Denver, parting ways was always bittersweet.

"Lehigh Valley or…" Saunders' voice trailed off. Talking about the options a failed platoon player might have was an awkward conversation for an established guy to initiate.

"Denver. GM swung a deal with the Rockies." LeGrande continued packing his belongings, which prevented him from seeing the look of relief on Saunders' face.

"You'll hit some bombs out there."

"Yeah, buddy." LeGrande thought back to the two-run blast he hit several weeks earlier. No matter his role in Denver, he hoped there were plenty more of those moments ahead of him with the Rockies as the season headed toward its midway point.

"I'll make you some of my famous spaghetti when you're back in town – I think we host the Rockies in August." Saunders paused before cracking a wry smile. "A shame we'll have to sweep you right out of Philly."

"We'll see about that." The two men shook hands, embraced, and headed down different paths. Saunders to the batting cage, LeGrande to Philadelphia International. He would meet up with his new team in Atlanta, and with the redirection to another roster, he could feel the anxiety that had gripped him like a vise all season begin to fade away. "See you when I see you."

"See you when I see you, brother."

14

Change of Scenery

"Remind me to fly the next time I'm traded." Behind a flood of red taillights, Tyson Jackson crept along I-95 toward a date with his new ball club in Philadelphia. The travel secretary for his former team, the Pittsburgh Pirates, offered a puzzled look when Jackson had asked for a rental car in lieu of the short flight from Baltimore where the team was wrapping up an interleague series against the Orioles. Jackson figured the drive would be faster. He figured wrong.

"Traffic that bad? You've still got time to get there before the game, no?" Jackson's wife, Desiree, did her best to focus on the positive. She always did.

"I talked to the manager, a good dude named John McGown, after Ulrich told me about the deal. I'm coming off the bench tonight anyway." Jackson had heard about McGown from a few of his teammates in Pittsburgh and by all accounts, he was a straight shooter – a player's manager who valued hard work and expected his veterans to lead by example. At this stage of his career, that's all Jackson wanted. "Lefty on the bump tomorrow. McGown said I'd be in the lineup."

"That's great, honey. It's nice to know these things ahead of time."

"It'll be different, that's for sure. My A-Bs will take a hit in Philly." Jackson had started most games for an injury-riddled Pirates team through the middle of June. Getting full-time at-bats, though refreshing for a guy who spent much of his big league career as a part-timer, had served the dual purpose of also confirming his limitations. He was on pace to amass career highs in several categories, but playing every day also revealed his drastic platoon splits for all the world to see. Against lefties, Jackson had hit a robust .312 with six home runs in 61 at-bats. Facing righties, the numbers left little doubt that his team would be best served benching him: a .169 batting average with no extra base hits. His Jekyll and Hyde performance presented an all-world stat line juxtaposed against a complete horror show. Jackson enjoyed playing every day, but doing so had, in a way, proven to be his undoing.

"Look on the bright side." He loved that his wife always managed to find the silver lining in everything. "You've always mashed lefties. You may not play as much in Philly, but when you do, you can make a real impact."

"McGown expects I'll get a few starts every week, a handful of pinch-hit appearances too. It'll be a straight platoon." Desiree had a point even if the move from Pittsburgh was bittersweet for the couple who had grown to love the Steel City. McGown was putting him in a position to succeed; the percentages were in his favor. Plus, it didn't hurt that his new team was on the doorstep, just a couple games out of first place. Meanwhile, the Pirates languished at the bottom of the Central Division. "He wants me to be like that cat, Valentín – remember him? A chemistry guy."

"Yes, of course! I thought he was one of the coaches." While she had only met Marcel Valentín briefly during the second baseman's pit stop in Pittsburgh a couple years prior, he had left an impression.

"McGown thinks I can be a guy who can lead by example."

"That sounds about right for my man." Desiree took a deep breath and reflected on their journey in the big leagues. From the joy that came with her husband being on every top prospect list to the disappointment when he fell short of those lofty expectations at the highest level of pro ball, they had seen it all together. This would be a new experience, a new challenge.

"I've never really thought about myself in that way. I've always just kind of fought for playing time and tried to hold onto my spot with everything I've got."

"I think that's the point, honey." Desiree could see what McGown and the Phillies saw in her husband, even if he couldn't quite understand it himself. "You know what it takes to make it in this league. They have some young guys – be a teacher. Be a leader. It comes naturally for you; I know it does."

Jackson considered his wife's words carefully as the road ahead opened a bit and the realities of a fresh start in Philadelphia drew nearer.

"A new chapter."

"A new chapter. You'll do great."

———

The rain started coming down mid-afternoon and by 5 p.m., it hadn't let up. There would be enough of a break around first pitch, however, for the Phillies and visiting Cardinals to get the game in without incident. The players would be the first to tell you that a rainout off-day is not quite the same as a scheduled off-day. It was a break from the physicality of playing baseball, but pre-game routines, mental preparations, and rituals can also take a toll. Even if the first pitch crossed the plate after midnight, it was better than the alternative. Few in the clubhouse ever prayed for a rainout.

Jackson made it to the ballpark just as late-afternoon sunshine broke through the cloud cover for the first time. He took it as a good omen – both for his future in Philadelphia and for the team's chances on a soggy night.

"Mr. Jackson, welcome to Philadelphia." A security guard at the main gate greeted the team's newest addition with a warm smile and a strong handshake as he pulled into the lot off Pattison Avenue. "Players' lot is to the left. Pablo will show you the way just ahead."

"Appreciate that… Ernest." Jackson leaned forward to read the man's name tag. He liked to get acquainted with the people in and around his home ballpark and his arrival in Philadelphia felt like the first day of school all over again. "I'll be seeing you around."

Jackson passed hordes of fans, many shaking out umbrellas and peeling off their raincoats with the arrival of the summer sunshine. Few gave a second look to the black Mercedes creeping past tailgates and whiffle ball merriment. Philadelphia loved its sports stars, but this hard-scrabble fan base wasn't star-struck too often.

Though he had played in Philadelphia quite a few times in his career, the stadium held a newness for him that he hadn't expected. The feeling would fade the first time he dug his cleats into the dirt at home plate or ran across the left field grass. For now, however, he allowed it to linger. He was excited; his chest filled with the kind of nervous anticipation he recalled experiencing just before his big league debut. After a decade in The Show, it was a refreshing twist on his usual pre-game mindset.

"Hey, hey – look at this Yinzer over here!" Barrett Taylor was the first to rise from his clubhouse card game to greet Jackson with a term of endearment common in Pittsburgh in case the newcomer was feeling homesick for the Steel City. If Jackson had any intention of slipping into his new role quietly, a packed clubhouse, on account of the weather, made that notion moot. "Nice to meet you, brother. Welcome aboard."

"Excited to be here," Jackson canvassed the room and smiled at the new faces looking on from every corner. Familiar faces here and there, but the newness of the experience remained. "Even more excited to be off the interstate."

A few laughs from his new teammates, but mostly, it was business as usual for the young ball club. That suited Jackson just fine. In short order, he would grow comfortable in an unfamiliar clubhouse and a brand-new city rich with history and in love with its sports teams. He would adapt to his new surroundings and soon, that clubhouse, at first so foreign, would become his home away from home. On this night, he'd watch the action from the bench, making it as far as the on-deck circle for a potential pinch-hitting opportunity before marching back to the dugout without a plate appearance. The next night, facing a tough lefty, he'd go two for three with a run-scoring triple, setting the tone for a win in his Phillies debut. The nervous energy subsided quickly and before the series ended, he was just one of the guys again, doing whatever he could to contribute to a winning ball club. The excitement – the thrill he felt on his first night at the ballpark – stayed with him, however. He was writing his own story in a new city – a new chapter in a book not quite half-over, the climax several months down the road. By the end of June, he had helped the Phillies leapfrog the Mets for the first time and climb into first place. The tale yet to be told, as always in the mid-summer months, remained a mystery.

15

A Star Arrives

"I know it sounds strange, but it's a weird feeling not being part of it this season." The ball hit Tanner's mitt with a pop. He took a few steps back, waved his arm like a windmill, and launched the baseball back to his throwing partner, Bennett Peterson.

The All-Star Game had become an annual tradition for the young hurler since he broke into the big leagues four years earlier. After beginning the season with the worst month of pitching in his young career, Tanner would most assuredly miss out on the Midsummer Classic for the first time. Of course, an argument could be made that leaving him off the roster put too great an emphasis on what he did the first month of the season rather than what he had done in the more than two months since. After a rough April, Tanner turned his season around in May and June, recording a 7-1 won-loss record against an equally sterling 1.81 earned run average. His secret? For the first time in his professional career, he let go. Tanner had a hard time hiding how much his April struggles bothered him. Ever the perfectionist, he wanted to erase his unsightly earned run average and reverse the mounting losses with every start. Of course, it doesn't work that way. Normalizing stats after a bad start takes time. Tanner felt pressure to turn his season around and because of that, every pitch

96

became a chore and post-game interviews became mentally exhausting. And so, he stopped paying attention to the numbers on the back of his baseball card and just pitched, results be damned. He stopped pressing on the mound, stopped trying to be so perfect. And then, a funny thing happened: once he stopped trying to be perfect, Tanner's performances were nearly just that. He had transformed back into the pitcher everyone expected him to be. And although the turnaround may have come too late for All-Star voters, Tanner and the Phillies put more weight on what it might mean come October. "I'm not going to know what to do with myself."

"Do what I do," Peterson replied before grunting with the release of another long toss. "Sleep."

"I'm not sure you'll have the chance this time around, Ben. They might still come for you yet." Tanner stepped back again until the two men were hollering at one another to continue their conversation during a long toss session that now stretched from the left field foul line into deep centerfield. The comment reached Peterson's ears, however, and he couldn't help but shake his head and chuckle. Midway through the season, the best of his career, it was clear to all observers that Bennett Peterson had arrived.

All promise and no results as a pro, Peterson's career was on life support when he entered Spring Training as a long shot to make the Phillies roster. Under the tutelage of Pitching Coach Pedro Arroyo, the giant man with an electric left arm managed to harness his immense abilities that spring and at the season's halfway point, the results were undeniable. Pitching in a team-high 43 games, Peterson had evolved from his "LOOGY" role (in baseball parlance, the "lefty one-out guy" label meant that he had been trusted throughout his career to face left-handed batters almost exclusively). Now, a few months into the season, Peterson had emerged as the lights-out setup man everyone hoped he could become, striking out 71 batters in 40 innings against just nine walks. Truly, with bragging rights on the line in the annual All-Star showcase, the National League could do worse than Bennett Peterson.

"Not a chance." He unfurled another toss before pulling off his glove and jogging across the vast outfield to his teammate. "They don't like to take relievers without those gaudy save numbers."

"I don't know, man. What you're doing is hard to ignore," Tanner replied. "I think you and your lady might have a fun week in Seattle ahead of you."

"Would you believe that after all of the traveling I've done in this game, all of the different leagues, all of the minor league assignments, I've never been to Seattle? I'll get there one of these days." Their work done for now, Peterson put an arm around the Ace, a baby-faced cherub compared with the grizzly bear standing at his side. In the late innings of close games, the team had come to rely heavily on the rubber arm and intimidating presence of their grizzly bear.

John McGown stood in the shadows where the tunnel to the clubhouse meets the dugout. He enjoyed these quiet moments at the ballpark before the crowds poured into the stands and the dugout came alive with activity. It was during these times that he often reflected on the team's performance and visualized his players executing that evening's game plan. Some people meditate; others listened to music or hit the gym to clear their mind. McGown filled his with baseball.

It was also in these moments that he enjoyed witnessing the otherwise unseen intangible of clubhouse chemistry manifesting before his eyes. A hot topic on sports talk radio shows and among fans everywhere,

McGown believed in the value of a healthy clubhouse culture. In an era of advanced analytics and pressure to quantify everything, he didn't need numbers to know that a happy player was a productive player. He watched with arms crossed as Aaron Tanner and Bennett Peterson, two of his shining stars, walked across the field together, deep in conversation. You can't force friendship, but McGown craved this kind of camaraderie for his players.

"You guys looked good out there." He clapped his hands and ascended the dugout steps to meet his pitchers on the warning track dirt. "Nice and easy, huh?"

"All coming together, Skip." Tanner gave Peterson a fist bump and nodded toward his manager as he passed and disappeared down the ramp.

"Ben, come on down to my office. I'd like to have a few words with you." The big lefty turned to his manager with surprise painted on his face. "It'll only take a sec."

Peterson ducked his head as he passed through the doorway that led to McGown's office and the clubhouse. His heart raced with every step. It's not every day that a manager asks for a one-on-one, and in Peterson's experience, those conversations hadn't gone all that well in the past.

"You've had a good season, Ben. Real good." McGown leaned back and crossed his arms while addressing his steady reliever. "You're on some kind of roll."

"I've had a nice little run so far." Bennett squirmed in his chair, only holding eye contact briefly before turning away again. His mind raced as he searched for a reason, any reason at all, why his manager might pull him aside. "Got my good stuff working and it sure is nice to settle into a steady role."

"Well, whatever it is, people around the league are starting to take notice, son." *Here it comes*, Peterson thought. While his early season success had caused the lefty flamethrower to grow more confident on the mound, Peterson still wasn't a glass half-full kind of guy. Years of disappointment had conditioned him to expect the worst. "Let me ask you: how well do you know Joe Stanley?"

"I know he managed the Dodgers to a World Series win last year, though I can't say we've ever met." Peterson's nomadic big league experience and adventures on the waiver wire hadn't yet brought him into the Dodgers' minor league system or Stanley's dugout. "Forgive me, but my head is spinning right about now, Mac. Why are we talking about Joe Stanley?"

Peterson couldn't handle the suspense any longer. As a bullpen arm, he recognized his role within the machine: a replaceable part in the machinations of a big league ball club. Through the season's midpoint, he had delivered solid results for the first team that ever gave him a real shot. Still, he wasn't blind to the fact that sometimes, teams cash out early when an overachiever finds a little success. Seated in the principal's office, Peterson feared his Cinderella story was about to take a detour.

"Well, Joe and I have been friends for years and he gave me a call this afternoon. Do you know why?" McGown tried to suppress a smile. It was clear to the old manager that Peterson was sweating bullets. What the pitcher didn't know, however, was that McGown was about to make his day. *Making the kid squirm a little might do him some good*, McGown thought.

"I haven't the faintest idea. Have I been traded?"

"Traded? You think I'd let Mark ship you out of town without a fight? Hell no, son," McGown said with a smile. It was time. "On account of the Dodgers' success last year, Joe has the privilege of managing the National League All-Stars. He's looking for a shutdown lefty to come out of the pen and help the team win. Does that sound like anyone you know?"

"I have a few ideas." Peterson exhaled and fell back into his chair with relief. He would still be on the move, but his midsummer flight was destined for Seattle rather than Los Angeles.

"You're an All-Star, kid." McGown reached across his desk to shake the big lefty's hand. "The boys planned a little ceremony for you after the game tonight – act surprised. Why don't you go ahead and call your wife. This is news she's gonna want to hear."

Peterson raced back down the hall and catapulted himself onto the field again, soaking in the warmth of the midday summer sunshine. High above the field, well above the right field line, he could make out the forms of two or three teammates running stairs together. Tanner, back on the field beneath the shadow of the left field foul pole, jogged over to Peterson when he saw him emerge from the dugout.

"What did the old man have to say?" Tanner tried to suppress a smile; he, like everyone else in the clubhouse, knew their reliable reliever would be christened an All-Star. Still, he wanted to hear the man say it himself.

"I'm an All-Star." The words sounded so strange, so foreign coming out of Peterson's mouth. For so many years, he just wanted to be able to say, "I'm employed." This All-Star business was something new.

"I know. Everyone knows. It's been in there all along, my man." Tanner gave his teammate a fist bump before retreating down the dugout steps and into the tunnel. Muted replays from the previous night's game played on the stadium's massive scoreboard. The only sound in the ballpark was the din of highway traffic a mile or two to the east. Peterson kicked at the dirt around home plate – an unfamiliar place for a late-inning reliever. He traced his cleats along the outline of the plate that he had mastered so beautifully for half of the season. The journey, however, had been much longer. And all along, right by his side, Abigail had been with him through the rollercoaster ride. His victory, his All-Star selection, also belonged to her. He had called her many times to share news through the years – most of it bad. After years of disappointment, years filled with painful phone calls to his biggest advocate and his closest friend, this was one call he couldn't wait to make.

16

The GM

"Is he calling my desk line or cell, Marci?" The summer months were always busy for Mark Johnson, GM for the Philadelphia Phillies, and this season was no exception.

"Desk line. Shouldn't be more than a minute."

Some people attributed Johnson's high success rate in free agency and windfall of high-performing, high-ceiling prospects in the draft to a keen understanding and use of the advanced analytics synonymous with the game today. Others believed it was his willingness to listen to the insights brought forth by the team's scouting staff. Johnson knew it wasn't so simple. From the beginning, he committed to considering everything – trend data from his most highly educated Ivy League analysts alongside the least scientific report from his most road-weary, old-school scout. He wanted to understand the trends hidden in data, but he also wanted to know whether a high school shortstop had soft hands and quick feet. If you have access to perspectives and context about everything, why discount anything?

The phone rang and Johnson turned from the window where he had been watching the groundskeepers tidying the edges of, in his estimation, the most beautiful infield in baseball.

"Johnson."

"Hi, Mark. It's Ruben." Ruben Almora, GM of the Houston Astros, remained as close a friend Johnson had outside of the organization. As close as rival GMs could be, anyway.

"Rube, how's my favorite Texan?" Johnson loved to bust Almora's chops about the job he had accepted in Houston. Several years earlier, as two star-crossed newcomers chasing the big league dream with middling front office jobs in Boston, Almora declared that he would never work for one of the league's Texas franchises. Why? He never did share the reasoning for his vitriol for the Lone Star State, but in a fitting twist of fate – perhaps the work of the fabled Baseball Gods – Almora enjoyed a two-year stint as an assistant general manager with the Texas Rangers before ascending to his current position further south.

"Hotter than hell. The scary thing is that I've grown to love it. How about you? Boo birds chase you out of Philly yet?" Ruben could dish out a good barb just as well as he could take one. It only made Johnson appreciate the man that much more.

"Oh, come on now. They love me here." Johnson laughed before transitioning quickly to business. The trade deadline loomed at the end of the month and now was not the time for idle chitchat. "Tell me, what can I do for you?"

"We could use a reliable lefty in the 'pen."

"You and everyone else. What did you have in mind?" These were the types of conversations he would need to have for the next several weeks, even if most wouldn't result in a deal. Johnson was certain his old friend had Bennett Peterson on his wish list, and they both knew that the big lefty wasn't going anywhere. Still, you never know where these conversations might lead.

"Peterson?"

"We like him." Part of the fun of these conversations was predicting which names might come up. So far, Johnson was one for one. Then again, he always could read Almora like a book.

"We do too." Almora laughed as he spoke; it was as if he had anticipated the answer he'd get from his old friend. Of course, he had to try.

"What's not to like?"

"It's incredible, really. His transformation has been astounding." While Johnson and Almora were peers competing against one another for the same precious resources, their friendship allowed each man to acknowledge when the other had made a wise move. "I'd say you got lucky when you plucked him off the scrap heap, but that wouldn't be fair. That was a stroke of genius, Mark."

"I have a good team and I get good intel. We saw something in him, and we didn't allow his past results to cloud our judgment."

"Well, it was an under-the-radar move last winter and it looks brilliant today," Almora continued. "Kudos."

"Thanks, old friend."

"I call it like I see it," Almora replied. "What about Brashear, the kid in Triple-A? He's blocked with the big club, no?"

"Trolling for prospects now? We like him. He's got a big future ahead of him when his time comes." At this stage of the process, still a couple weeks away from the All-Star break and nearly a full month from the trade deadline, most of Johnson's calls followed a meandering path. He used the term "trolling" with Almora and in truth, the process was quite a bit like fishing. Dangling a few names out there, trying to get a bite. Almora had been honest – the Astros could use a shutdown left-handed reliever to sure up a leaky bullpen. And if you have the GM of the

Phillies on the line, why *not* ask about Brashear? Of course, this call, like many others Johnson would have in the next few weeks, was never going to lead to a deal. Almora was gathering information, determining player availability for the next call or perhaps the call after that. By the time July 31 rolled around, he, like many other GMs across the league including Johnson himself, would have collected enough information to separate realistic trade partners from those without the complementary pieces that a deal would require.

"I'd say his time could come pretty quickly with the Astros," Almora said. While Philadelphia was content to take their time with the team's top prospect, Brashear would most likely find himself in the Astros' infield mix the moment any hypothetical deal was struck. "If he's off the table, where does that leave Dolan? He's got another year left on his deal, right?"

"He does. We like him – and before you give me shit, yes, I know I sound like a broken record." In truth, Johnson liked the whole 26-man roster, down to the last guy at the end of the bench. After swapping Richie LeGrande for Tyson Jackson a couple weeks earlier, he expected that the Phillies might stand pat at the deadline – that is, refrain from making further moves. Of course, there was no sense broadcasting those intentions, regardless of the depth of his friendship with Almora. "He's been splitting time with Valentín, they're both playing well and I'm not one to mess with something if it's working."

"Fair enough."

"I could use a little pop behind the plate." Now, it was Johnson's turn to probe. Rick Toperick brought Gold Glove caliber defense to the catcher position, but he was a liability with a bat in his hands. Acquiring a little extra punch to slot in at the bottom of the batting order, even as part of a platoon with the sure-handed Toperick, was worth considering. Of course, Johnson would tread lightly. Reducing Toperick's playing time might spark an uprising among the team's young arms that had come to rely on the veteran to guide them through the perils of pitching in the big leagues. Meddling with a formula that had worked into July was a delicate situation to navigate. "What would it take to pry Sammy Butler away?"

"We think his ceiling is pretty high." During these early conversations, it behooved Almora to play it coy. "He could hit 20 to 25 bombs with regular at-bats."

"That may be so. Of course, you and I both know you're not going to give him regular at-bats – not with that glove," Johnson said.

"I'll admit that he's a work in progress; there's room for growth, though. Sammy has a big league arm and our metrics suggest his defense is coming along." Almora was holding the line, as Johnson expected he might. It didn't make much sense to wilt at this stage. "He's going to be a hell of a catcher in this league and I don't think it's going to be too far down the road."

"Hey, if you like him, you like him." Johnson looked at his watch. The fast-paced life of a big league general manager left little time to dwell on deals that wouldn't happen any time soon. "He might fit what we're trying to do here, so let's keep a line open on the young man."

"I'll do that. Always a pleasure, Mark." The call crested the 10-minute mark and in that time, Almora had collected detail on four players – Peterson, Brashear, Dolan, and even Valentín. All unavailable, but it was useful information to stash away in early July, nonetheless. For Almora, it was time to turn his attention to the Phillies' minor league system to see if any combination of prospects would make a deal for Sammy Butler palatable. He doubted it, but general managers never say never. "Holler when you're down here after the break."

"You can count on it. You owe me a beer."

"I'll have an ice-cold Shiner Bock waiting for you. In the meantime, stay in touch if you want to do business."

Johnson hung up the phone and returned to admiring the field, a tapestry of bright green grass set against a rich red clay infield. It's often said that fandom fades when the game becomes work. Johnson never found that to be true. He loved baseball and imagined he always would. Somehow, it's during the hot summer months in South Philadelphia, when the ball flies off the bat, the grandstands are packed to the gills, and the trade season begins in earnest, that he falls in love with the pastime of his childhood just a little bit more.

17

The Prospect

Crack!

The echo of bat meeting ball ricocheted off empty seats as Mike Brashear sent a pitch over the right field fence.

Crack!

Another quick swing, all wrists and torque, and another offering from the Lehigh Valley IronPigs' bench coach soared beyond the wall – this time, dead center.

Brashear kept his eyes trained on the next pitch as it approached the plate, reloading quickly after lifting another ball toward the left field foul pole and into the humid Lehigh Valley air.

Crack!

A line drive landed inches off the right field foul line and just inside the first base bag.

Crack!

Another liner, right up the middle.

Crack!

Dig in, swing, and reload. A would-be double skipped past the third base bag and settled at the base of the wall in left.

"That'll do for today." Bench Coach Rod Cleary looked at his watch. Six o'clock. "Day game in Harrisburg tomorrow. Get some food and rest up."

Mike Brashear rested the bat against his legs and removed his batting gloves while replaying the after-hours batting clinic in his head. He surveyed the quaint field, which stood still apart from Cleary's movement off the pitcher's mound. Brashear didn't say a word, but he didn't have to say anything. Cleary knew enough about his second baseman to know that while his work at the plate was finished for the day, it would continue for hours between his ears – constant visualization and mental fine-tuning of one of the minor league circuit's most big league-ready swings. That Brashear had sprayed each pitch in order around the diamond – first beyond the fence, second as scorching liners across the infield dirt – was no accident. Once pigeon-holed by scouts as a raw talent with dramatic pull tendencies at the plate, Brashear put in the extra time to become the least predictable hitter in the league. Truly, he had developed the ability to place the ball just about anywhere he wanted. Some called it a gift, but the young man everyone called "Brash" attributed his evolution to hard work and good coaching.

"Thanks for the extra tosses." Despite his quick rise through the team's minor league system and sky-high ceiling, Brashear carried himself with an unexpected dose of humility. Some called him old-school, a grinder who only knew how to play the game one way: all-out. Brashear had a different perspective: he was just a baseball player who hadn't yet made it to The Show. Every day presented an opportunity to get better. He didn't expect that mentality to ever change, whether he was riding the buses in the minors or flying charter flights in the big leagues. It just wasn't in his DNA to approach the game any other way.

Mike Brashear had baseball in his blood. His father, Mike Senior, played a decade as a utility infielder for the Detroit Tigers and his grandfather, Warren, enjoyed a few cups of coffee across a 20-year career in pro ball, spent mostly in the minors. To say that the youngest Brashear possessed the highest potential for greatness would be an understatement. As a child, he took to the game quickly. While being the son of a big leaguer meant that his father wasn't around much during the baseball season, the younger Mike gravitated toward the middle infield positions in fond imitation of his old man. As he matured and a future in the game looked to be a reasonable goal, the two men were inseparable during the long, cold Detroit winters. Father and son would lose track of time taking swings in one of Detroit's finest indoor batting facilities from the first snowfall to the spring thaw, and talk baseball from sun-up to sundown. The training routine wasn't always so traditional, however. The elder Brashear was an old soul; he believed that hardship and trials built character and toughness. So, it was with that in mind that the two men would leave the comfort of the cage for the blistering cold of the outdoors and a game of pepper atop the frozen landscape of the city's outer sprawl. What's a little frostbite to a baseball-obsessed teenager? You haven't lived until you've laid out in a foot of snow to snag a screaming liner. For Brashear, the challenge during these drills remained the same each winter: pluck that little white pill, hard as a rock on account of the sub-zero temperatures, out of the air before it disappeared forever in the glistening snow. The preparations, extreme by some measures, made him tough. Once spring brought the rest of the region's aspiring athletes out of hibernation, those extra preparations turned him into a superstar. Even today, several years removed from the Little League and high school exploits of his youth, a billboard bearing his likeness beneath the words "Home of Legendary Plymouth Superstar Mike 'Brash' Brashear," welcomed visitors to his hometown just outside of Detroit.

"Talk to your pops lately?" Cleary handed Brashear a towel as the two men slipped into the quiet locker room, palatial by Triple-A standards but a few notches below the luxurious accommodations provided by big league clubhouses.

"Just about every day. Always talking my ear off about something I've done down here – for better or worse." Brashear smiled at the thought of his father's constant chattering. Ever opinionated, the elder Brashear still loved talking baseball many years removed from his playing days. "He can't help himself. I love the old man, even if I can't ever get a word in edgewise."

"He used to do the same thing to me back in our play-ing days – my God, that man loves to talk!" Cleary let out a belly laugh as he reminisced about his long-time friend and occasional teammate. He played with Brashear's father for a few years during a short stopover in Detroit before Cleary moved on to longer tours of Cincinnati and San Diego. "He has a good mind for the game, but I'll be damned if he could keep his mouth shut for five minutes. Always talking, always talking. Give him my best."

"I sure will." Brashear peeled his workout shirt off and stuffed it in his duffel bag. Time was too short to concern himself with a proper shower and a change of clothes, so he headed out into the early evening shadows in a t-shirt, uniform pants, and flip-flops. "See you in the morning, Rod. Thanks again."

———

The bus ride to Harrisburg from the Lehigh Valley – Allentown, Penn., to be precise – wasn't among the worst in minor league ball: an 80-mile trek, mostly high-way miles along I-80. Most of Brashear's teammates used the time to catch up on sleep. Some read while others fiddled with their smartphones. Brashear? He studied. One lesson he learned early from his father was the value of advance scouting. When a batter steps into the box, he has a split-second to identify the pitch coming his way and decide when to swing – if at all. Rather than wasting his idle time, Brashear preferred to huddle up at the back of the bus with his tablet, reading up on the pitchers that waited for him at the end of the journey.

The ballpark in Harrisburg was just like any other at the Triple-A level: quaint and family-friendly. As he made his way out of the visitors' dugout and onto the field to warm up before the 1 p.m. start, he couldn't help but notice the swell of bodies situated in the seats about eight or nine rows behind home plate. Mostly men, mostly middle-aged, all with notepads in hand.

Scouts.

"Hey there, Mike. Becca Stoyanos, I write for the Philly Voice. We met in Clearwater." Hers was a familiar voice. During an eye-opening experience with the big league club in Spring Training, he had become a curiosity for a few of the Phillies' primary beat writers. Among them, Becca Stoyanos.

"Of course, I remember. Great to see you again." He was surprised to see her in Harrisburg given the Phillies had a big series at home against the rival Mets. "Didn't expect to see you in Harrisburg today – what gives?"

"Marco's got tonight's game in Philly. I'm covering these guys." She pointed to the men seated behind home plate that had caught Brashear's attention moments earlier. "It's that time of year, Mike. A half-dozen or more scouts at every minor league game. I have a good handle on who they're with; the trick is to figure out who they're watching."

"We've got a lot of guys who can help a big league club, that's for sure." Brashear fixed a resistance band beneath his feet and continued his pre-game routine while he spoke with Stoyanos. "I love my teammates, but it's tough because you want to see them get their shot."

"That's the nature of the game. Something tells me this might be a quiet deadline for the Phillies." Stoyanos looked toward the group of scouts and recognized Sam Melvin, a highly respected scout for the Phillies. If Melvin was here, Stoyanos imagined, he was here for one reason and one reason only: to evaluate Brashear's development. Where Sam Melvin went, promotions often followed. "I think they might also be keeping an eye on you today, too – not to add any extra pressure on you, of course."

"There's never any extra pressure." Brashear looked up at the crowd and smiled. "I approach it the same way, every day. Just go out there and give 'em a show."

"I should get back to the press box. Good luck, Mike. Hope to see you in Philadelphia before too long." Becca and Brashear shook hands and he returned to his rituals. The preparations for every game remained the same, day in and day out. For a moment, however, he allowed his mind to drift to a time when he would step to the plate, not in one of these low-key minor league ballparks, but that roaring complex on Pattison Avenue in Philadelphia. If he kept playing the way he had been playing, it wouldn't be long. Of course, it wasn't his decision to make. All he could do was prepare, put in the extra time, and force the Phillies' front office to make the call by playing the game the only way he knew how. In the meantime, no sense worrying about what he couldn't control. He'd be ready when they decided he was ready. Until then, he'd embrace the Harrisburg day games, Lehigh Valley nights, and every bus ride until his last.

18

The Sound of Summer

"It's a beautiful night for baseball in Philadelphia. Hello, and welcome everyone to another exciting evening with your Philadelphia Phillies." Leonard Pries' baritone filled the radio waves with a familiar refrain across the Tri-State area. "We have a terrific match-up to bring you tonight as the young ace, Aaron Tanner, faces off for your first place Phillies against Kyle Greenleaf of the New York Mets."

Following in the footsteps of broadcasting legend Harry Kalas, Pries had served as the Phillies play-by-play man for going on 25 years. Seated to the left of color analyst Henry Lorenzo for 20 of those years, Pries and his partner provided a degree of consistency in the radio booth that Phillies fans loved. Truly, for most of the region, Pries and Lorenzo provided the soundtrack to the summer.

"Not a cloud in the sky on a hot summer night and I'll tell you, Henry, it doesn't get much better than this." Pries had a natural way of bringing his color man into the mix. For those tuning in at home or on the road, listening to Phillies baseball was more like eavesdropping on two poets deep in conversation – or painters describing their work in vivid detail. An argument could be made that there was no finer pairing in all of baseball than Pries and Lorenzo.

"You said it, Leonard. A slight breeze out to right, though I can't imagine that'll be too much of a factor tonight." Lorenzo brought an energetic quality to his commentary, the excitable fan to Pries' soothing, straight-forward reporting. Each man a perfect complement for the other. "Tanner has really turned his season around after a rough start and though he won't be pitching next week in the All-Star Game, he has bigger goals in mind, and they all lead to October."

"As you alluded to, Henry, we are indeed a few short days away from the Midsummer Classic and this game tonight has definite implications. Both teams, neck and neck in the NL East, would like to head into the break with a series win."

"That's right, with a win, the Phillies can move three games up on their rivals, but a loss shrinks the lead to just one game over the Mets." Phillies fans understood just how important these games were, of course. But the job of the broadcaster is to paint a complete portrait of the action on the field and everything surrounding it. "It goes without saying that you want to head into the break with a little momentum for that second half playoff push."

"And the Phillies will try to do just that when we come back from a short break." Pries was a pro when it came to telling stories in short bursts, filling airtime with just the right amount of content before switching gears deftly. "We'll run down tonight's lineups and keys to the game on the other side."

Pries surveyed the field and etched a few notes in his scorecard while local commercials aired in the back-ground. Keeping score of each game had been a hobby of his throughout his career in the booth. During the offsea-son, he lived in Arizona with both his wife of 35 years and a lifetime of memories from calling games. Tucked away in a small study, he kept a bookshelf filled with notebooks of completed scorecards dating back to the late-1980s. Every entry was an intricate series of letters, numbers, and colors – a foreign language to most, but for the veteran broadcaster, the games burst to life again when he pored over each dusty notebook. His wife, Janet, often caught herself entranced by his proficiency for pulling a random notebook off the shelf, from say, May 1992, and reciting for her a memory from an otherwise unremarkable game. He would describe a play that stood out for him in such detail, perhaps a sparkling defensive gem, that it was like being back in the stadium calling the play all over again. And for his wife, her husband's words were so descriptive, so perfect for the moment, that she couldn't help but close her eyes and watch the play unfold in her mind – even if she couldn't quite recall the play that he described. He was that good. "Here's a good one: Remember that time Jackson ranged to his left and tracked Myers' ball down in the sixth? What a beautiful play; he was always so fluid in the field," he'd ask her. No. No, she most certainly did not remember that play or most of the others that he would recite as if he was pulling it right from last night's game notes. But that was what made Pries so special for Phillies fans across the region – storytelling was an art and Leonard Pries was a master.

"Henry, did you see what the young gun in Lehigh Valley did last night? Brashear?" Pries said. Though not a household name across the country, the recent exploits of Mike Brashear had become difficult to ignore for Phillies fans and, likely, the team's front office. "Hit two more rockets. Every time I see him, he barrels up the ball better than any youngster I can remember."

Committed to a productive platoon between Ryan Dolan and veteran Marcel Valentín, the team was not expected to move either man at the trade deadline. Dolan was a consistent contributor, if not a little rough around the edges, a little prickly. Valentín, however, had a reputation as a "glue guy" – meaning that in addition to playing an important role on the field, his true value came from contributions out of the public eye. Like glue, many believed his presence on the roster held the clubhouse together. While Dolan's solid batting line wasn't much of a surprise, Valentín's on-field performance had become a fun little story itself. After puttering in and out of the league for the better part of a decade, he had come into his own, batting .297 with a healthy mix of extra base hits in part-time duty. It may have taken more than a few years for Valentín to stick in the majors, but he never dwelled on past cuts and demotions. Better late than never. The logjam at second base made it more and more apparent that the team was willing to take its time with Brashear, the young man many hoped would grab ahold of the keystone position for the next 15 years. For now, the future would have to wait.

"He's unbelievable. As much as I'd like to see him in red pinstripes, they're playing it safe with him and you can't argue with the approach." An old-school mind, Lorenzo seldom advocated for moving prospects through the system too quickly. "The kid'll get his shot soon enough."

This banter between two old friends was nothing new for Pries and his booth partner. That it occurred off the air was even less surprising – Pries and Lorenzo never cared much about saving their breath. They were always game to talk baseball.

The evening's game progressed as expected, with two promising hurlers trading zeroes. Philadelphia broke through with two runs in the fourth, but the Mets answered with two of their own in the sixth. In the bottom of the eighth, Jose Alvarez gave the crowd reason to cheer, and for Pries, it was a chance to serve as narrator for a night the young man from Cuba would always remember.

"Two and one the count now to Alvarez. He sets, winds, and the pitch… dribbled foul, down the third base line. Two-and-two." Pries always leaned forward when the Cuban sensation stepped to the plate. Whether it was the flamboyance with which he played the game or his propensity to deliver in clutch situations, the mild-mannered import had not disappointed in his first taste of the big leagues. "The 2-2 pitch… low and outside. Full count to Alvarez, Taylor waiting on deck."

"If you're McGown, you'd like to see Alvarez show some patience here with Barrett Taylor's big bat coming up behind him, but if he gets his pitch, he can do some damage against this righty." Lorenzo's right foot tapped violently beneath the desk as it often did while he awaited the payoff pitch. Short of a foul ball, there was destined to be some action in the ballpark with the next pitch and it always sent excitement coursing through his body like an electric current.

"The payoff pitch… ripped down the left field line and it's going to go all the way to the wall!" Pries' voice rose like a wave surging toward the shore while Lorenzo slapped his hands together, though he had the presence of mind to keep his celebration quiet enough to avoid detection on the airwaves. "Alvarez is off to the races – the ball skips off the base of the wall! It gets away from Jaffey! Alvarez digging for third, they're going to wave him home! The throw to the plate… the slide… not in time! It's an inside-the-park home run for Jose Alvarez, the first of his career, and it puts the Phillies ahead three to two! Can you believe it?"

"I can't. Unbelievable!" It was not uncommon for Lorenzo to be rendered speechless by these moments of chaos on the field, but that's what made their partnership so special. Pries, the master narrator for the unfolding drama, and Lorenzo, the beating heart of the fans. Three outs later, the Phillies had preserved another win and

Alvarez received a pie to the face for his heroics. Typically reserved for walk-off winners, the playful veteran catcher, Rick Toperick, made an exception and surprised Alvarez with a face full of shaving cream on account of the first home run of his career – and an unconventional one at that.

The game ended, wrapping up the first half of the season. For Pries and Lorenzo, the All-Star Break represented an opportunity to recharge their batteries for the season's home stretch, and work on their golf game. This night, however, was far from over. After the final sign-off of their radio broadcast, both broadcasters stepped in front of the camera to join their television counterparts for a roundtable discussion about the game action and its stars of the night.

"Hi there, Leo. Nice call tonight." Victor Allegro, seated on a stool with a handful of notes, greeted Pries as he arrived for the post game show. "Good to see you too, Henry."

"Thanks, Vic. You gentlemen looked as good as ever in high-definition tonight." Together with Victor's color analyst, John Harrison, all four broadcasters enjoyed the chance to team up for the post-game wrap-up at the end of a long day. As the months passed, they'd only get longer as the marathon season careened toward its finish line.

Another hour would pass before Pries could make his way around the corner from the ballpark to his apartment – home away from home during the long season. As the city fell quiet, Pries replayed his call of Alvarez' home run in his head, analyzing his description like a pitcher might review his mechanics or pitch selection. He was a perfectionist and wanted to do right by the athletes on the field, the fans listening at home, and history revealing itself in the moment. The call, in his estimation, was good. Not quite to the standard that he had set with Aaron Tanner's first career no-hitter the previous season, but a good call, nonetheless. Before too long, his eyes closed, his mind had cleared, and Pries drifted off to sleep. Recollections of the game's pivotal moments faded, replaced by dreams of the days to come, dreams of home.

19

Star-Crossed

Bennett Peterson stood out in a crowd. Even among superstars, it was hard for the quiet giant to fade into the background during the All-Star Week media day hosted near Pike Place Market in Seattle's bustling downtown. He arrived in town as one of the National League's best stories at the season's midpoint and while no one would mistake him for one of the league's big money stars, he had locked down the late innings as well as anyone in baseball through July. Relievers are, by virtue of their assigned roles, one dimensional, but for three-and-a-half months, Peterson had mastered his dimension better than anyone in the game.

Nothing beats the morning before the All-Star Game for first-time participants like Peterson. He mixed and mingled with fans, took photos with his more famous All-Star teammates, and met with media at a simple, skirted table bearing his name in big block letters. It was all so surreal for the journeyman reliever who was making the most of what, a few months earlier, he thought might be his last chance. What kind of market would there be for a 30-something reliever with a half-dozen stops along his big league journey, most of them mediocre at best? It was Philadelphia or bust back in Spring Training. Prior to reporting to Clearwater for the exhibition slate, he had privately explored what the job market might hold for a baseball washout with a high school degree and a couple years of college courses to his credit. A midsummer trip to Seattle as a representative of the best performances the National League had to offer was an unexpected and much-preferred alternative to what a future without baseball might have held for him.

It was here in Seattle that he was confronted with an often-repeated question as the hours of media appearances passed by: What changed?

That was the question on everyone's mind about the big lefty no one would have invited to the party a few months earlier – the big lefty who now sat alongside the best players in the game. Several reporters asked if he had adjusted his mechanics. Some commented that his fastball seemed to have more life on it. Still others wondered if it was less about Peterson's improvement and more about better catching.

Nope, nope, and nope.

So then, what changed?

Most reporters left their conversations with Peterson a little underwhelmed. There was no way the solution to his issues on the mound could be so simple, they would say. Not for this guy, not for the guy who couldn't throw a strike to save his life. For years, Peterson ping-ponged between Triple-A and the big leagues, grabbing ahold of a job just long enough to disappoint, just long enough to frustrate another coaching staff and find himself back on the bus to the minors. His Philadelphia story, however, was something different. And it all started with a Spring Training conversation with his manager, John McGown.

It wasn't even what McGown said that led to his transformation on the mound. Rather, it was the trust the old man placed in his pitcher that made all the difference.

Finally, after so many chances that ended in failure, and countless managers and front office personnel left shaking their heads at the unfulfilled talent wasting away in Peterson's left arm, it was McGown's unshakeable commitment to the young man when he was at his most fragile that turned his career around.

"Not the way you expected to spend July, huh?" Through the crowd, Mark Dorfman appeared in front of Peterson's table.

"Thought I'd be fishin," Peterson deadpanned, but it wasn't too far from the truth. "It's good to see you, Mark."

"You too – an All-Star, can you even believe it?" Dorfman understood better than most how improbable Peterson's rise from the ashes had been. After the team plucked the big lefty off the waiver wire, the league's communal scrap heap, Dorfman spent a considerable amount of time with the man through the ups and downs of his offseason journey. As a columnist for the *Delaware County News*, he had chosen Peterson as his subject for an ongoing series of feature stories through the dark and cold winter right up through his road to redemption, which culminated in April when Peterson made the team's Opening Day roster. The story since then, notable for its high points rather than any low lights, had pretty much written itself.

"They keep telling me I'm on the team. Not sure I'll believe it until I'm sitting in that dugout with 'National' written across my chest." Peterson was often self-deprecating, but his performance left little argument about his All-Star worthiness. "If I'm being honest with you, it's a dream come true. Never would have expected this for myself in a million years."

The two men exchanged a few words while Dorfman scribbled notes along the way. On assignment, he'd be required to log a dozen stories before the cross-country flight home in a few days. It was fitting, then, amid the pomp and celebration for the league's larger-than-life superstars, that his first call of duty was a follow-up piece on the least likely superstar of them all. The Phillies sent three players to Seattle – not a total to sneeze at, but the fact that the Mets, a team looking up at Philadelphia in the standings, sent six to the Midsummer Classic was a reflection of the Phillies' subtle greatness through the season's midpoint. Sitting atop the NL East division, three games ahead of the New York Mets, most experts expected a second-half letdown. A few players were playing over their head and as fun a story as the Phillies had been through mid-July, consensus among people who talk about these things was that they were still one or two pieces short of playoff contention. There was no shame in a late-season fade for the first-half Cinderella story, they'd say. And yet, as Dorfman liked to point out to the national writers less familiar with the day-to-day happenings in Philadelphia, the team brought a comfortable lead into the dog days of summer. Why couldn't it continue? He wasn't a fan – as a beat writer, you check personal rooting interests at the press box door – but he had seen enough Phillies baseball to hold onto some optimism that he'd be covering baseball in October. And if not, he had no doubt that the team would be in the thick of the playoff hunt right to the bitter end. So, no. After three-and-a-half months of first place baseball, he was not ready to dismiss the team's early success so easily.

"Hey, Mark, good to see you." Another Mark, Phillies GM Mark Johnson, stuck his hand through the crowd of reporters gathering around the league's stars and toward Dorfman for a handshake. "You see Peterson yet?"

"I sure did. Like a deer in the headlights." Dorfman and Johnson chuckled at the thought of the star-struck reliever enjoying the first taste of his own stardom. Media day at the All-Star Game can be overwhelming for the uninitiated. "You can't help but feel good for the guy. It's quite an honor."

"It is. He's really come on this season – he's made our team better." Johnson scanned the room, looking for his counterparts from around the league. It wasn't lost on Dorfman that amid the excitement of the All-Star break, some players changed addresses. It was just the nature of the beast: get enough general managers together in one place and players are bound to find new homes. "I'm glad the league took notice."

"You've got the trade deadline coming up in a couple weeks – think it'll be a quiet one?" Dorfman couldn't help himself. When you have a private moment with one of the team's top decision makers, sometimes an interview breaks out.

"I do. I really do." Johnson understood how these exchanges worked and he tried to be open and approachable with the press – to a point. Dorfman had been in the game long enough to recognize how far he could push the GM and when it was time to back off. "We brought in Jackson last month to play left field for us and he's done everything we've asked him to do. The starters, specifically Tanner, have come around. We like our team."

"Any fear some of these guys are playing over their head? Valentín comes to mind," Dorfman wasn't alone in wondering if Marcel Valentín, enjoying the best season of his career, might come back to Earth as the season continued on.

"There will always be some of that – some regression. I don't worry about Marcel, though. He's a professional and he's getting an opportunity this year to show what he can do with a consistent role," Johnson said. Valentín's impact off the field had been a topic of much debate in the press box between Dorfman and his contemporaries. While few would argue against the veteran's leadership qualities, its impact on the team's results in the standings was hotly contested. Dorfman, ever the optimist, tended to think there might be something to it.

"From where I sit, it's been fun to watch." Dorfman pointed toward the sky, a reference to the Phillies' press box that rested high above home plate. "More than a few good stories on this ball club – not the least of which is sitting at a folding table soaking in this spectacle right now."

Conventional wisdom suggested that this would be Peterson's crowning achievement, that he was among the overachievers who might slide toward the finish line after the break. But what if he didn't? What if he had, in fact, harnessed his immense talent and emerged on the other side a completely different pitcher? If that was the case, Dorfman thought, this story had only just begun.

———

Three days after he sat among the National League All-Stars, answering questions from reporters, many who had never heard of him, it was all over for Bennett Peterson. Surrounded by the league's best, he expected to be little more than a decoration seated at the far end of the bullpen bench during the exhibition itself. A knick-knack, an oddity on a roster filled with superstars. Instead, Joe Stanley, manager of the Dodgers and the National League All-Stars, walked to the mound in the bottom of the sixth inning and tapped his left arm to indicate a call to the Phillies' big lefty warming in the bullpen. Peterson entered the game with runners on first and third, and the challenge of retiring two tough lefties in a game led by the American League, 5-1. Six pitches later, he was back on the bench, two three-pitch strikeouts on his All-Star stat line, and millions of onlookers across the country asking, "Who's that guy?"

It was a picture-perfect night despite the outcome, an 8-3 loss. And then, just like that, it was over. He boarded a flight to Philadelphia, signed perhaps a few more autographs than usual on the other side, and readied himself for the stretch run.

20

Abigail

The morning hours were never easy.

Her alarm clock was a ticking time bomb that manifested at unpredictable hours in the form of a three-foot tall cherub. She never knew when it would startle her from her dreams; the only thing she knew for sure was that it would be unpleasant. A tap on the forehead, a thumb in the eye. Whichever way she was poked and prodded by her impish toddler, Abigail Peterson could count on the morning to bring a rat race of activity before the world slowed down again just before noon when her daughter mercifully tucked in for a nap. Not quite a single mom on account of her marriage to a nomad named Bennett, the life of a baseball wife sure carried with it some similar experiences. Life had been good for the couple, particularly this year, but the mornings were hard – and hardest during her husband's long road trips.

The second half of the season began with a two-week swing through the Midwest and for a mother hoping to instill as much normalcy in her toddler's life as she could manage, the hotel hopping and air travel became problematic once the little girl's summer activities began in earnest. Nowadays, Abigail and Bennett chose one longer road trip each summer where the family could be together and, aside from his responsibilities to the team, treat the road trip like a mini vacation. During the day, they would visit the city's zoo or on West Coast trips, enjoy a day at the beach. At night, mother and daughter would join the Phillies' other traveling families supporting their boyfriends, husbands, and fathers. This summer, thanks to Bennett's surprising All-Star selection, they agreed on a policy change and made it two long road trips. It isn't every day that a little girl gets to watch her father play baseball among the best players in the world.

"He did well in that game, didn't he?" The voice on the other end of the line belonged to Abigail's mother.

"He sure did."

"That ought to be worth a new contract, don't you think?"

"Mother, he's just taking it one game at a time," Abigail replied with a hint of exasperation. Her mother had the best of intentions, even if she struggled to understand the intricacies of big league contract negotiations and Abigail tired of trying to explain. "He has a good agent – Seth will make sure he gets a good deal after the season. There's no sense talking about it."

"I just think they owe it to him – and you – to give him some security. I know how hard it is for you both when the next contract is hanging over your head. It's not right." While misguided, her mother wasn't wrong. A little security *would* be nice. For the Petersons, the journey to big league success had followed a winding route with few guarantees that a big payday, or even just the faintest notion of job security, would ever come. During his sporadic big league experiences, Peterson had endured a litany of setbacks that threatened to kill his big league dream before it truly began. On several occasions, he had been cut loose after receiving a non-roster spring training invitation. Another time, he was unemployed for four months after surviving Spring Training roster cuts until the final day of camp. The only consistency in his career was inconsistency, the trauma of life as waiver wire fodder year after year. Now, for the first time, the light at the end of the long tunnel drew nearer. Of course, you can't allow thoughts of that next contract to enter your mind – not now, not ever. Abigail knew that the moment her husband concerned himself with anything that came next, aside from the next pitch to leave his hand, what seemed a safe bet would surely dissolve before their eyes.

"Right or wrong, Mother, that's just the way it works." Abigail was ready for another topic. "He has a few more months to go. If he continues to pitch the way he has so far, I'm sure it'll work out for us. Who knows, maybe they won't even wait that long."

She would never admit it, but she was growing more and more nervous as the season progressed. Her husband's All-Star appearance was a high watermark in a season that had gone better than anyone could have imagined. But cracks had begun to show in his first few outings since. Game after game, the old habits reappeared – a few walks, a couple hit batsmen. In three short appearances, all lasting just a few batters, he had given up four runs. When you've allowed four runs in the previous three-plus months, any hiccups stand out a bit more than they might otherwise. When your track record resembles those hiccups more than the successes, well, it's easy to understand why anxiety levels in the Peterson household might be on the rise. Fortunes change quickly in baseball, however. Heading into August, he seemed to have returned to form, striking out five of the six batters he faced across two appearances. For Abigail, she could only hope he had gotten the yips out of his system. For the next 10 weeks, she would be the picture of poise; burying her fears somewhere deep beneath the surface. Of course, it wasn't all an act. She always believed in her husband's ability. However, now that he had shown the world what he could do, now that they stood on the precipice of everything they had ever dreamed about during those many hard days and nights toiling away at the grind, she knew how much a few extra years – and zeroes – on that next contract might mean for her family. And how fast it could all slip away.

At least this time, she thought, it seemed logical that he'd be in the same uniform for the entire season. She couldn't remember a season when she had lived in the same home in April and October. Would she still live in Philadelphia, a few doors down from Amelia Tanner, her best friend and the wife of Phillies' ace Aaron Tanner, next April? Only time would tell.

————

Bennett Peterson had a love/hate relationship with getaway day. Getaway day, the universal term for the final day of a road trip, meant that he would be sleeping in his own bed later that night, next to his wife and down the hallway from his daughter. Getaway day also often meant the team played midday baseball, and every now and then, he would even make it home in time for dinner. Of course, getaway day demanded early mornings and uncomfortable suits. Peterson hated early mornings and he sure as hell hated wearing suits.

"I'll wear this damned thing because it's the rule, but I still haven't heard a good reason why we need to sit on a plane for six hours like we're going to a business meeting." Peterson voiced his disapproval to the one man he figured might feel his pain, his brother in burliness, Phillies' larger than life first baseman Barrett Taylor. "I quit school because I didn't want to dress up for business meetings."

"That, and you were a pretty good ballplayer," Taylor quipped. "I hear you, brother, but we make these suits look good, B.P. You gotta roll with it." Taylor was always a bit more easygoing than most. He often looked on the bright side of situations and if he was forced to shove his body into an expensive pinstripe suit, he'd make the most of it. "I think I'm going to add a little razzle-dazzle on the next trip. Maybe a bow tie to class it up a bit."

"Think Mac will let me rock a tuxedo T-shirt? For the sake of the team, I mean." Peterson paused to load his luggage onto the team bus before boarding. "It's a win-win for everyone: I wouldn't have to wear a suit and there would be one less big sweaty guy dripping all over the plane."

"That's an idea I can get behind." Taylor followed Peterson up the stairs, and both men settled into aisle seats halfway toward the back. Little by little, the bus filled up. Some talked with one another, others read. It was a short ride to LAX followed by a long flight to Philadelphia International. Aside from his displeasure about the team's required getaway day attire, Peterson left California in a better mood than when he had arrived two weeks earlier. After a rough stretch, he rediscovered his groove and left LAX with confidence, helping the team take two of three against the defending World Champion Los Angeles Dodgers – including a hard-fought 3-2 victory on the final day of the road trip. Thanks to the series win in LA, the team survived the grueling 10-game road trip with an even split and were itching for some home cooking and a long home stand to make up some ground. The Mets had closed to within a game-and-a-half during the same two-week stretch. The beauty of divisional battles in baseball was that nothing had ever been decided before August. To that end, the two rivals still played one another 10 more times before the season's final day. For Peterson, he had worked his way through his first struggles of the season and headed home refreshed and renewed – energized for the first real pennant race of his big league career.

21

Standing Pat

The trade deadline had come and gone. Mark Johnson sat at his desk in quiet contemplation, enjoying a moment of peace that followed weeks of phones calls and intense negotiations. For the first time in a long time, his phone no longer rang. And for the Phillies, the trade deadline slipped by without incident. It was neither an overwhelming success nor an abject failure, as the team that would enter the month of August looked awfully similar to the team that picked up a win on the final day of July. Johnson entertained dozens of prospective deals – some offers were enticing, though most fell well short of consideration for the man at peace with the idea that the best move may be no move at all.

Standing pat at the trade deadline was sure to ruffle a few feathers among the team's fan base, and the fallout of his decision to hold steady would be felt perhaps more broadly than that. Cable sports programs had already debated the pros and cons of the Phillies' perceived inactivity. Meanwhile, local sports talk radio hosts were ready to eat Johnson alive, as many pined for a big splash to cement the team's status as a surefire contender. That the pieces Johnson collected during the offseason had come together well enough to maintain a slim division lead had little bearing on the fans who clamored for action. And therein lies the critical difference between the desires of a rabid fan base and the needs of the team's front office to balance present day fixes and future success. Was there a deal out there that might have catapulted the Phillies from surprising success story to World Series favorites? Possible, though not probable. If there was, Johnson was certain no GM brought that winning deal to the negotiation table. He had made it clear that he wouldn't deal productive players off of the big league roster, and most offers from the rest of the league centered on a few blue chip prospects he couldn't rationalize moving. The way Johnson saw it, any proposed trade offered incremental improvement today for potentially devastating steps backward in the years to come. For the "win now" diehard, the all-in approach might sell a few more tickets, but Johnson knew it wasn't the key to sustained success. Or to keeping his job.

Johnson left his office and jogged downstairs toward the clubhouse. If there was one man within the organization he wanted to regroup with after the deadline passed, it was Phillies' manager John McGown.

"What do you say, John?" McGown, glasses low across the bridge of his nose, waved his GM in without looking up from his paperwork. On a few sheets, Johnson recognized heat maps outlining the hot spots and weak points of a player whose name he couldn't quite make out. On another, a lineup card with a few cross-outs and notations scribbled across the page. McGown was a workaholic – always grinding, always trying to improve his team. Johnson was cut from the same cloth, though cast in a vastly different role. "I can swing by later if you're tied up."

"My door is always open to you, Mark. Just wrapping up a few things."

"The deals just weren't there this year, John. I tried like hell to get you a few extra pieces." Johnson wouldn't go so far as to apologize because there wasn't any need. McGown was an old-school baseball man. He knew the drill. At the deadline, you try to make a move to help your ball club get better. You never make a move just to make a move. It was because Johnson held McGown in such high regard that he wanted to give the man a chance to ask questions or share his point of view on useful pieces that might become available later in the season as teams shake a few players loose following their own trade deadline maneuvers. The trade deadline may have passed, but there would still be opportunities to improve the team.

"We have a good ball club." McGown wasn't just trying to offer his GM reassurance. He believed the team could win as constructed, as it had done for four months. "If you got it right in the offseason, why meddle?"

"Jackson has adapted well to Philly – that's a move I'm glad we made." Johnson had traded for Tyson Jackson in mid-June, well before the deadline dealings occupied his every waking moment. During the six weeks that followed, the left fielder fell into a productive platoon that solidified an area of weakness. No one would write volumes about Jackson's performance, but no one would complain about it either. "His price would have been through the roof had we waited until July."

"That's the way it goes," McGown replied. "Tell me, who were the hot commodities this time around? It always interests me who the rest of the league falls in love with."

"Brashear. Can you even imagine? He's easy to dream on, but the return just wasn't there." Johnson didn't need to plead his case. McGown had seen enough in the blue-chipper to know they had something special on their hands. "If we dealt Mike, I think we'd live to regret it in a few years' time. Maybe sooner."

"If you ask me, he's untouchable." McGown had high hopes that when the team determined that the young man had squeezed all the knowledge and fine-tuning he could get out of Triple-A, he might spend the rest of his career patrolling second base in Philadelphia.

"About as close as it gets in this game." Johnson nodded in agreement. Assuming he stayed injury-free and continued to manhandle Triple-A pitching, Johnson was sure Brashear would earn his first cup of coffee in the big leagues before the season ended. "Peterson came up a lot too. Everyone's got their eyes on the big lefty."

"I can see that. He turned some heads at the All-Star Game." McGown leaned back and crossed his arms as an idea popped into his head – something he had hoped to discuss with Johnson for some time. "Think we might lock him up before the offseason? Couldn't be more dominant in those late innings and I'd like to give him some peace of mind. I don't call the shots here, but the kid's earned it."

"He's an interesting case." McGown couldn't argue with his GM even if it wasn't the answer the old manager hoped to hear. Peterson's career suggested a regression. On the other hand, there wasn't another arm in his bullpen McGown trusted more with the game on the line. "The question is one of consistency, right? Can he keep it up or is he due for a fall?"

"He's been a rock for us. Some guys are late bloomers. I'd like to think he can be a key part of what we're building for the next few years."

"I'll exchange some numbers with his agent." Johnson had played it coy to manage McGown's expectations, but there was never a doubt that the team would try to extend their most unlikely success story. The question now was whether the values assigned to Peterson by his team and himself were within the same figurative ballpark. "We'll get a sense of what they're thinking and try to keep him off the open market. Give him that peace of mind he's earned."

"I'd like that, Mark. Thank you, kindly."

Johnson stayed a while longer and, in time, the conversation steered away from the game and the business of the game. Before too long, they had fallen back into the familiar routine of trading ideas about offseason fishing plans, comparing notes about winter golf destinations, and, as a nod to their fandom for the city's other sports franchises, what moves they might make to put the Flyers over the top in the National Hockey League. Amid the grueling summer months of the baseball season, playing fantasy general manager of a team in another sport always proved strangely energizing. In these moments, they could be fans again. An odd pairing, Johnson and McGown had developed a strong bond thanks to a combination of factors – namely, shared interests outside of the baseball world and a shared desire to win another World Championship for their employer. Lost in conversation, it wasn't until much too late that both men realized it was time to bring one day to a close and prepare for the next one.

"See you in the morning, John," Johnson said through a yawn. "Heading toward the finish line."

"We are indeed."

"Keep me apprised of anything you think might help us down the line – you know I appreciate your input." It was true. While some of his contemporaries kept their field managers at arm's length when it came to personnel decisions, Johnson never saw any reason to exclude the man who knew the team's players best. "I'll do whatever I can do to help us get better."

"I like our guys, Mark. Noted, but I like our guys."

"We can ride this thing out and see where they take us. It's my job to look for upgrades; just let me know if you find yourself wanting for reinforcements." Johnson headed down the hall, out of the building, and into the darkness of midnight in South Philadelphia. Not a soul to be seen in any direction, aside from an empty, out of service bus and an occasional car creeping along back alleys near the ballpark. As much as he enjoyed the other local teams that shared the hearts and minds of the region, Johnson loved the midsummer months of the baseball season most of all: a time when all eyes cast their gaze on the city's little gem of a ballpark on Pattison Avenue. The basketball and hockey seasons were long over. Somewhere to the west of Philadelphia, the Eagles were taking the first snaps of training camp, though the new football season remained somewhere beyond the horizon line. For now, the Phillies continued to capture the imagination of sports fans across the city. Sports talk radio hosts often proclaimed Philadelphia a football town, but Johnson believed nothing compared to the Phillies' faithful fan base. He just hoped that the team he had resurrected from the dead just a few years earlier could give the city, his adopted home, the championship it so desired.

22

A Strange New World

Even in a strange place, one that he had only just begun to understand, the familiar crack of the bat always made Jose Alvarez smile. The sound was no different here than it was anywhere else he had played. The crackle of polished maple against a tightly wound baseball served as his touchstone when he needed it most – no foreign languages to decipher, no confusing customs to master. Just bat meeting ball, ball leaving bat. Amid all the new experiences, there was always that sound to keep him grounded in his first season away from home. Away, for the first time, from Cuba.

"Otro." *Another.*

On a humid day in August, Alvarez sprayed baseballs across the outfield lawn of his home ballpark, pausing between each fluid swing to watch the ball land between a couple of outfielders engaged in small talk or follow its path to the base of the wall, or over it. It was an off day, but for Alvarez, that just meant more time to perfect what many believed was an already perfect swing.

"Otro." *Another.*

A switch hitter, Alvarez moved to the right side of the box before the next practice pitch arrived at the plate. His swing, compact and quick, was smooth as butter anywhere he stood in the box. Nearing the end of his first season in the most competitive league in the world, pitchers were still looking for a weakness in the young man's game. The oldest cliché in the book proclaims that baseball is a game of adjustments. Ballplayers must continually evaluate and adjust their approach as pitchers identify weaknesses and adapt to strengths. Through the season's first 100-plus games, Alvarez had little reason to change his approach at all. His fluidity at the plate had earned him the nickname "The Natural" after Robert Redford's character in the classic film bearing the same name. The game came easy for Alvarez. But then, it always had.

The youngest of five brothers, all ballplayers at one time or another in Cuba's Baseball Federation, Jose possessed the potential for greatness at a young age. Growing up in Santa Clara in a modest bungalow beneath the city's imposing statue of revolutionary Che Guevara, Alvarez tagged along at his brothers' games for many years before stepping foot onto the playing field himself. As a youth, he would bring water to the players and run mid-game errands as circumstances required. He would do anything to help the ball club – anything to be close to the sights, sounds, and smells of the game he loved. Sometimes, he was asked to run into the stands to deliver messages to players' girlfriends. Other times, he would leave the ballpark to collect postal deliveries or pick up snacks at a nearby market. He was a jack-of-all-trades as a child, and it wasn't long before he grew into a master-of-all-trades on the playing field.

You can argue that baseball was, in many ways, a family business for the Alvarez clan. At least, it was in their blood. With few exceptions, it's what Alvarez men had done for the past 100 years. The family archives are filled with scattered memories and stories of mostly modest performance in the island nation's pro leagues. Of course, stories of modest performance quickly evolved into tales that stretch the boundaries of truth. That was never the case with the young Jose Alvarez, however. His performance never required embellishment. He was, for a short time, Cuba's biggest star.

For American baseball fans, Cuba was an island shrouded in mystery for many decades. Stories of prodigious performance became legend across the U.S. as Major League Baseball received an occasional import in the form of defecting Cuban ballplayers. Some Cuban athletes lived up to the lofty expectations foisted upon them by strangers in a new country while others foundered beneath the pressure. Together, they all shared the common bond of enduring hardships along the path to the big leagues that would be hard to grasp for most players traveling more conventional routes to the majors. Each defection carried with it harrowing tales of escape, though most players who managed to reach the U.S. border and earn that first big league contract tended to keep the trauma of the journey to themselves during the early days in a new country. Separated from family, all communication severed for years at a time in some cases, it was easier to simply focus on baseball.

Times had changed since his great-grandfather played a variation of the game Alvarez played now. And more recently, times had changed since his father wrestled with the temptation of fleeing for the big leagues when Alvarez was a child, ultimately deciding that the risk to his family was too great. He gave up the big league dream before it started and continued to play and manage on Cuban soil. His greatest joy? Living long enough to see his youngest son thrive on the sport's grandest stage.

Talented athletes like Alvarez now found much smoother passage between Cuban shores and the United States. In fact, for Alvarez, the transition from Cuban megastar to Major League rookie was a simple one in comparison to his predecessors. After a home game in Santa Clara, notable for his two home runs, two stolen bases, and a highlight-reel defensive gem, his manager introduced him to a scout and the rest was history. Three weeks later, he signed a four-year contract with a team he had only passing knowledge of and a city he knew nothing about. There were jokes about cheesesteaks – something about a giant, cracked bell. No matter. Major League Baseball represented a new challenge for the easygoing Cuban – a new adventure, and a new contract that would set his entire family up for life. If after four years the big league life didn't work out for the young man, he could still count on returning home a conquering hero. Indeed, times had changed for Cuba's baseball stars. The world's opportunities lay well within reach.

In Philadelphia, Alvarez found everything about the American baseball experience to be a more polished version of the game back home. The grass was greener, the infield dirt tidier. The media circus took some getting used to, though little by little, he adapted. Though he missed home, home wasn't quite as far away for Alvarez as it had been for the Cuban defectors of years' past. He could always go back, though as the season pressed on, he only felt the slightest pull of Santa Clara, and even that faded with time. One thing that he simply couldn't get used to made itself known around sundown each day. If there was one area of his new life in America that he struggled to adapt to, it lived in the kitchen: he had yet to find anything that compared to the food back home.

"Eso es todo." *That's it.*

Alvarez dropped the bat head to the dirt and pulled off his batting gloves, nodding to the mound where Juan Fernandez, Phillies third base coach and resident Cuban adjustment counselor, stood behind protective netting. Fernandez left Cuba the hard way nearly a half-century earlier and had been tapped by McGown to help shepherd Alvarez along his American journey. Some might mistake Alvarez for the quiet type, but it's easy to forget that the man was learning a new language and a new way of life on the fly – a new everything. Hernandez had encouraged him to connect with his non-Spanish speaking teammates in other ways while he gradually picked up the basics of the English language. And so, it was with that in mind that the young man introduced his new clubhouse to a weekly song and dance competition at the beginning of each new home stand. In lieu of deep conversation, dance and (mostly terrible) singing served as his way of expressing himself, his personality, and his culture. It was quirky, it was embarrassing, but it worked. More importantly, it was *him*. Baseball, despite a demanding 162-game season, presents its athletes with plenty of idle time. Alvarez had found a productive new way to fill the moments in between the action, and build a few bridges to his teammates along the way.

———

"He's got quite a swing, doesn't he?" Tom Flanagan of the *Philadelphia Inquirer* called out to Hernandez from above the dugout as the latter hopped off the mound. "Reminds me of another Phillies infielder who should find himself in the Hall of Fame these next couple of years."

"Nice and compact, quick to the ball. Not hard to see a little Chase Utley or Jimmy Rollins in there; harder to find anything to complain about." Hernandez tilted his head toward the empty press box above home. "What are you doing at the yard today? Doesn't that fancy paper of yours ever give you a day off?"

"You'll have to talk to my editor about that," Flanagan quipped. "Just catching up with Leonard. You know he's been doing play-by-play now for 25 years? Thought that was a worthy story for a quiet news day."

"Twenty-five years, Lord have mercy." Hernandez couldn't help but contemplate what he was doing a quarter-century ago. "I think I was riding the buses down in Lakewood back then. Low-A, my first coaching gig."

"I won't even tell you what I was doing." Flanagan was a respected veteran in the press box, but Hernandez still had quite a few years on him. "You've got a few more years in this game than I do. And I'll leave it at that."

"Okay, young man. You take care of yourself. See you tomorrow." Hernandez laughed and disappeared into the dugout. He enjoyed these unexpected, impromptu conversations with other men and women with enough passion for their jobs to show up on an off day and turn it into a workday. He saw in Flanagan much of the same appreciation for the craft of writing and reporting that he carried into his job as an instructor on the playing field. Based on what he read, passion poured through in Flanagan's writing. Much as he hoped his own passion would manifest in the form of the continued development of a young shortstop named Jose Alvarez.

23

Crunching Numbers

Approaching midnight on a Wednesday, you'd be forgiven for assuming that the Phillies' front office had closed its operations for the night. For the most part, you'd be right. The team was on the road and all non-traveling personnel had departed for the comforts of home several hours earlier. All, that is, but one.

The glow of a single computer screen casting its light through the window of a small office revealed one man who remained hard at work as Wednesday rolled into Thursday. Alex Corino, head of baseball research and analytics, was deep in thought and lost in the numbers.

He hadn't planned on spending the night at the office, but these things happen when you start digging into treasure troves of data. One statistic leads to another, which leads to another. And then, by adding those statistics together, Corino would find that he had created even more data points to explore. When data is your currency, it takes discipline to know when to wrap it up for the night. Corino would be the first to admit that he hadn't quite found that discipline since joining the Phillies' front office three seasons earlier.

He was part of an effort by General Manager Mark Johnson to surround himself with the smartest minds in analytics and scouting – an effort to buttress the team's player development and analysis capabilities with a healthy dose of science and cold, hard data. Johnson sought the perfect blend of soul and science: a strong scouting operation supported by formidable analytics. An infallible brain trust designed to build the perfect roster. That, of course, is the dream. Every team wants to fill its roster with players predestined to succeed, players that scouts and analysts agree can't fail. Ask anyone in the game, and they'll tell you it doesn't work that way. Baseball is a game of failure and it's a game of feel. For every player who follows success in high school, college, the low minors or wherever with success in the majors, there are hundreds, if not thousands, who fail to replicate past results without explanation. Sometimes, it's an inability to hit a big league breaking ball or an injury that never recovers fully. Sometimes, it's a matter of lost confidence. But often, it's unexplainable. They just lose the feel for the game. Corino knew there was only so much he could do to avoid these occurrences, but he could at least take some of the guesswork out of the rest of the player analysis process.

A ringing phone snapped Corino out of his hypnosis.

"Are you planning on coming home tonight?" It was his wife, Lucy.

"What time is it?" Corino looked through the blinds of his office window, which revealed only darkness. No sign of life in the office, either.

"Midnight."

"Oh, shoot. Sorry, Luce. I didn't realize it was that late." He meant it. So engaged with his work, he hadn't noticed the cleaning crew vacuuming and tidying hours earlier. He didn't notice when they yelled "goodnight" from across the office and he also didn't notice when the lights switched off. "I always lose track of time when I get into a rhythm."

"I know. It's okay, just come on home whenever you're done." Lucy Corino knew the drill. After five years of marriage, most involving the 'round the clock nature of a job in pro ball, none of this was new to her. Her husband had an admirable work ethic; she only wished he'd keep a closer eye on the clock.

"Okay, doll. I'm just wrapping up," he replied through a yawn. It's funny: only now, keenly aware of the time, did fatigue reveal itself. Had his wife not called, who knows how long he would have continued his analysis and calculations? His wife wouldn't have been surprised if he spent the entire night hunched over his keyboard. It wouldn't be the first time her husband watched the sun rise from a dew-covered stadium seat.

Many years ago, Corino sat in a statistics class at the Massachusetts Institute of Technology and wondered what the future held for him. He figured he would latch on with an analyst firm in the Cambridge area or perhaps build apps for one of the many software start-ups bubbling up in the region. Maybe he would even relocate to Silicon Valley, the beating heart of innovation just south of San Francisco. A career in baseball didn't make much sense back in those days. It's hard enough to break into the game if you don't stumble into an internship at an early age. It's harder still for the data scientist who, a decade ago, didn't have much of a place in the sport. For Corino, personal and professional passions didn't figure to blend. He'd graduate with honors from MIT and, separately, lose his voice cheering for his hometown Boston Red Sox. He was there in 2004 when the Red Sox shocked the world and broke an 86-year World Championship curse. He was there in 2007, seated along the third base line, when they did it again. Fandom attached itself to Corino in his youth and he feared that his career choices might steer him far from the game.

As luck would have it, many big league ball clubs started carving out a slice of front office real estate for people like Corino right around the time he took his final exams at MIT. A chance encounter with a member of the Chicago Cubs' front office led to a trusted endorsement for the young man on a quest to break into baseball's new data-focused frontier. A few years later, now holding a lofty title and shaping the process by which his team analyzes professional ballplayers, he was often amazed at just how wrong he had been to assume there wouldn't be a place in the game for number crunchers. It wasn't Boston, but it was baseball.

After the short call with his wife, Corino dipped back into his work for just a few moments. With a stretch and a yawn, he pressed his laptop closed and felt his way through darkened hallways. It had been a long day, one of many, but a day he hoped might bear fruit during the team's upcoming homestand against the Milwaukee Brewers and Cincinnati Reds. Studying player tendencies and reviewing rows and rows of numbers may be tedious to some, but in the numbers, Corino saw the full story. It wasn't just lines of data in a spreadsheet, it was, from Corino's perspective, irrefutable proof of everything unfolding on the field. Watch a batter a few hundred times with the naked eye and you might get an idea of his preferences. Corino's data, however, added a layer of validity to the informed speculation of performance evaluation. Does it appear that a certain player can't hit a low-and-away slider? Corino can prove or disprove that notion. Does a pitcher have more life on his fastball if he throws from a different arm slot? It's all in the data. Reading it, making sense of it, was Corino's gift to the Phillies. The Red Sox fan from MIT was now making a name for himself in the Senior Circuit (the common nickname for the National League, founded 25 years before the American League). Once certain his personal and professional lives would never intersect, he was now certain they would never come unbound.

———

"Jimmy needs to throw the hook earlier in the count." It was a few days after Corino's late-night cram session and the Phillies were home from a long road trip. This topic, a matter of pitch analysis, was the first of several hypotheses he intended to deliver to the team's coaches as the bounty of his most recent analyses. Some would stick with little disagreement while others returned to the "lab" for further study. Through it all, Corino was in his element holding court with the Phillies' coaching staff, though he had no illusions that his career path would ever lead him into the dugout. However, he enjoyed their company and felt he learned more from them than they ever did from him, even if it wasn't always apparent. These meetings, when he had the opportunity to contribute his discoveries and share perspectives with the men who led the team between the white lines, ranked among his proudest. "The whiff rate on his curve is 20.6 percent – that's fourth in baseball. He's been starting batters with the four-seamer most of the time, but he's been getting behind and when that happens, they're laying off the curve. It could be deadly for him."

"Let me see that." Phillies Pitching Coach Pedro Arroyo reached for a sheet of paper and studied the grid Corino had compiled to map the effectiveness of Jimmy Moore's arsenal of pitches. Moore, a steady presence in the Phillies starting rotation, was in the middle of another quietly productive season. Stepping up after the team had lost Daniel Baker for the season with a UCL tear, Moore had recorded a 9-6 won-loss record across 24 starts to go along with a 3.64 earned run average heading into mid-August. After reeling off 18 consecutive starts of six or more innings pitched, Moore's past few outings suggested that the wily veteran might be slowing down. This discussion was designed to refresh his arsenal and restart a new streak by identifying a strategy to utilize his out-pitch, a nasty 12-6 curveball, more effectively. "Well, I'll be damned. There it is. What do you think, John?"

"Talk to him. He's a professional. I think he'll be happy to mix it up." Phillies' Manager John McGown tugged at his glasses as he took a handoff from Arroyo and studied the data on his pitcher. "Twenty-point-six. Impressive. Good work, Alex."

It was another day at the office for Corino, one that followed another late night at his desk. The discussion with Arroyo, McGown, and the rest of the coaching staff led to small tweaks as the team prepared to host a couple of foes from the NL Central division. In a game of adjustments, you don't stick with one approach for too long. For the next few weeks, Corino would watch Moore's starts with a discerning eye to see if the emphasis on his curveball produced any incremental results. Of course, it would be foolish to expect that the league wouldn't counter Corino's insights with its own adjustments. So in a couple of weeks – maybe three starts, maybe four – a trend would emerge and the Phillies' chief analyst would be right back at the drawing board to find a new lever to pull, a new dial to twist. Whatever it took to help Moore keep hitters off-balance. The challenge, as always, was staying one step ahead. One step ahead of the league, and ahead of people like himself in rival organizations, analyzing every pitch and every play, every day until the last one.

24

A Bump in the Road

It was bound to happen at some point.

Aaron Tanner sat in front of his locker, a silent man in a silent clubhouse. He had pitched well enough to win, allowing two runs across six effective innings, but uncharacteristic defensive miscues proved to be the Phillies' undoing as they dropped their seventh game in a row, 4-2. And with it, the Phillies fell further into second place. The chasm between the team and the first-place Mets stood at two full games.

Until the team's recent stumbles, they were having the kind of season few had predicted and most perceived as a mirage. Among outsiders, success was viewed as the pleasant outcome of a bunch of decent players – spare parts on other teams – punching above their weight. Theirs was a nice story – cute, almost. But the baseball season is a marathon and anyone with an opinion outside of the clubhouse believed it was only a matter of time before the more imposing roster of the New York Mets flexed its muscle and raced past the upstart Phillies. In mid-August, those prognosticators were feeling quite vindicated. The Phillies, of course, didn't see it that way.

"The good thing about baseball is that it's easy to have a short memory." Anyone paying close enough attention knew Tanner hadn't always held that perspective. Mired in a brutal slump to begin the season, he had found it difficult to forget his failures. A nice little run of personal success made it easier to maintain perspective during the team's struggles. On this night, Tanner held court at his locker following the team's latest defeat. His hair was still wet from the shower, and bags of ice were taped snug against his right shoulder beneath rolls of elastic bandages to ease the recovery process. "We have a long way to go – how many weeks left? Seven?"

"That's right." Though he knew every beat writer by name, these post-game press huddles always caused him to experience a bit of amnesia. Responses and questions would come at him from every angle and he could never quite figure out where they were coming from. He was standing a foot or two away and he could hardly recognize their faces.

"A lot can happen in seven weeks."

"At what point do you start turning your attention to the Wild Card?" Another question volleyed toward him from the masses, a gaggle of bodies holding recorders and notepads, keeping their eyes trained on the young ace.

"Not on August 23, I can tell you that much." Tanner shook his head. He hated questions like that. "We have 35 games to go. If we start focusing on the standings with 35 games to go, you can forget the Wild Card and the division. We'll be on the damned golf course."

Since course-correcting his season after a slow start, Tanner had not once looked at the standings or his own statistics. When you're living the game day-in and day-out, you have a pretty good idea about how the season is going. Plus, there were enough people around him providing near-constant reports about the team's performance that he never saw any need to obsess about the numbers. For the first time in his career, he just let go. A creature of habit, and a superstitious one at that, when the results started coming for him shortly after he stopped analyzing every outing, he stuck with that plan and the results had been there ever since. For his team, however, the results hadn't been there for the better part of a week. Tonight's conversation with reporters had become all too familiar for the young ace during the team's slide, and while he gritted his teeth and endured as best he could, there was another man in the clubhouse who was having an even harder time moving on.

———

Ryan Dolan's return from the shower piqued the interest of a few reporters hovering around Tanner. It had not been a good night for the right-handed half of the Phillies' second base platoon. An above average, if not excellent gloveman, Dolan's walk back to the dugout at the end of the game had been the longest of all. His three errors, two leading to go-ahead runs in the sixth and eighth innings, were an uncharacteristic career-high and proved to be the team's undoing. He was better than that. His entire body of work across a six-year career proved that he was better than that. He knew it, and he knew the next game would represent another chance for a different outcome. Of course, as hard as he tried to push it from his mind, futility that dramatic sticks with you for quite a while after the game ends.

As he dressed, Dolan snuck a peek in Tanner's direction before turning away quickly. He admired his more polished teammate and wished he was better equipped to handle the team's recent struggles. Surrounded by reporters, Tanner deflected probing questions with a smile. *I couldn't do it*, he thought. No, Dolan was quietly unraveling. He knew he was next and if ever he wished to be invisible, now was the time.

"Ryan, a few words?" He closed his eyes and took a deep breath as a woman's voice hit his ears. She was the first, but it wouldn't be long before he was holding court for all the wrong reasons.

"Of course. Do what you've got to do." Dolan took a seat and leaned his head against the edge of his locker stall. In the moment, he didn't much care how pathetic and forlorn he must look to those puttering around the clubhouse. He'd straighten himself out once the local broadcast cameras migrated over to him; no sense exposing his misery to the fans watching at home. For now, he just wanted to be as comfortable as possible, though comfort in such scenarios is relative.

"It looked like the ball in the eighth took a bad hop – can you talk me through that play?"

"I just booted it. Nothing more to it than that – it hit the dirt and popped up on me, but that's a play I need to make." *God bless her*, Dolan thought. He appreciated that she had given him an out, but he'd make no excuses for his mistakes. It just wasn't his way.

"And in the sixth, was it the way Cruz approached the bag on the steal? Looked like you got crossed up a bit."

"I did. He was dead to rites there, as I'm sure you saw. Next thing you know, they're up two-one." Dolan rose to his feet as the crowd grew larger and the questions continued. He often lost patience with the repetitiveness of the exercise – after all, how many ways can you describe a screw up? Dolan wasn't a natural under the spotlight. His jaw tightened and face reddened amid the interrogation. He did his best, in the moment, to emulate his more well-spoken and polished teammates. Teammates like Tanner, the master of the artful postgame interview. It was a trait that ran through a handful of the men in the clubhouse, and he wished he was more adept at moving on from the struggles with a bit more tact, a touch more grace. What he did have in common with his team-mates was a sense of accountability, of owning up to his mistakes. Accountability bred trust and trust bred a club-house filled with ballplayers who believed in one another. Say what you want about the importance of chemistry, but the Phillies had it in spades. The only people unsurprised by the team's success up until recent days had been the 26 men in the clubhouse and the coaching staff guiding them through the schedule.

"Thanks, Ryan." The crowd dissipated, and reporters migrated toward the door to update stories filed moments after the game's final pitch.

"Let's do this again tomorrow." Dolan didn't spend too much time with the beat reporters on account of his modest role on the team. The beat writers who heard the comment turned back toward Dolan, waiting for the punchline. "I plan to hit three home runs tomorrow night to make up for the three miscues tonight – it'll be a better story for your papers."

Laughter filled the emptying clubhouse and Dolan turned back to his locker with a sigh of relief. While he joked about his future fireworks show, unlikely as it was, there was an ounce of truth in the statement. The end of one day brought about a chance for redemption with another game the next night. And with it, a chance to put an end to the longest losing streak of the season. A chance to push defensive blunders a little further in the rear-view mirror. A chance for a slap-hitting second baseman to hit three long balls? Sure, why not. Stranger things have happened. In baseball, you never knew for certain when the improbable, the spectacular, might occur.

25

Fight Club

It was the yelling that first caught his attention.

Phillies' manager John McGown had been at his desk, rifling through hand-written notes compiled during that evening's game against the Atlanta Braves. Another night, another loss. Another night trying to make sense of one more win that got away. Leading 6-1 in the eighth, an off-night for the team's relievers and another series of unfortunate defensive blunders by Ryan Dolan allowed the Braves to tie the game and force extra innings before sealing the comeback with a spirit-crushing three-run home run in the thirteenth inning. The loss, the Phillies' eighth in a row, spoiled a sparkling performance by the team's starter and sent the Phillies into the clubhouse on a sour note. In recent times, this was nothing new. And for Dolan, the mistakes continued to pile up game after game. McGown wondered what had gotten into his second baseman, but pushed the thought from his mind just as quickly. During a 162-game season, in a sport where even the best teams lose 40 percent of the games they play, no team is immune to struggles. No sense over-analyzing the ups and downs of a steady hand. That said, McGown noticed some alarming changes in a tight-knit clubhouse. Nerves had begun to fray and, as the shouts reached his ears, it seemed that heightening tensions had reached their boiling point. McGown lumbered down the hallway and arrived in the clubhouse to find a mass of players in various stages of undress – three or four of his players on either side of the fracas, trying to wrestle the big body of Tyson Jackson away from Dolan. The match-up gave him pause; in a fair fight, Dolan wouldn't stand a chance against the power-house left fielder. That was neither here nor there: there wouldn't be a fair fight or a fight of any kind on his watch or in his clubhouse. Not tonight, not ever.

"Knock it off, both of you! Cut that horseshit out!" Few had witnessed the steady old man lose his temper with his players. He had been ejected from his fair share of games for arguing with umpires, sure, but this was some-thing new for a young clubhouse getting its first taste of failure and it caused the commotion to mellow quickly. "Dolan, grab your gear and clear the room."

"Mac, I was minding my own damned business and he started rippin' my def –"

"I wasn't asking, I was telling." McGown, seething, looked toward the ground with his hands on his hips. Marcel Valentín, Dolan's platoon partner at second base and one of McGown's respected veterans, urged his hot-headed teammate to do as instructed and settle down elsewhere. Dolan packed a duffel bag hastily and walked away without a backward glance. He was right. It was the big left fielder Tyson Jackson who had tossed a few unpro-voked barbs at Dolan about his defense after another shaky performance. That, in turn, caused a quiet clubhouse to erupt into a volatile mix of pushing, shoving, scream-ing, and name-calling. In good times, player-to-player critiques might take the form of helpful, and welcomed, feedback. An "I noticed X, and you might want to try Y" kind of thing. And perhaps, under different circumstances, Dolan would have been open to suggestions about how he might fix his recent hiccups despite a body of work that suggested adequate defense as his greatest asset. But these were not good times and Jackson, a relative newcomer following a trade with Pittsburgh, hadn't read the room all that well. Dolan had been sulking at his locker, stewing about another missed opportunity to put an end to the slide. He was in no mood for a critical analysis, even if it was offered with the best of intentions.

"I meant no ill will to Ry, boss. I made a comment – a suggestion – and he snapped. How am I gonna let him talk to me like that?" Jackson's reputation as a never-back-down, hard-nosed player was one of the qualities that made him such an attractive trade target when the Pirates made him available. McGown just wished he had exhibited a bit more situational awareness. This was neither the time nor the place for a clubhouse scuffle. Not in the half-hour after a frustrating baseball game. Not with a couple dozen reporters with their ears pressed against the clubhouse door. "I'm not going to back down from anyone."

"Ty, that's not the way we handle our affairs here," McGown said. "I've got two-dozen reporters on the other side of that door. They're ready to bury us and I don't need to give them any more material for our eulogy. You're better than that. I'd like to see you cut the crap and show some better judgment."

"I get that, but –"

"End of discussion. Never again in my clubhouse, do you understand me?" McGown had been around the game long enough to know how to handle the different personalities that filter in and out of a big league clubhouse. Jackson might be a never-back-down kind of guy, but he had never battled wills with the John McGown. "You're here to be a leader. Start acting like one."

"Yes, sir. I got you." Jackson nodded and turned toward his locker with a deep breath. He hadn't expected to be of much interest to the beat writers on this night – an 0-3 batting line is hardly headline material. But now? Had the beat writers caught the melee from beyond the closed clubhouse doors, as McGown had suggested? Had he just created clubhouse chemistry issues? Sometimes, ballplayers argue. Sometimes, in the close quarters of a Major League clubhouse, tempers flare. Mounting losses and lost ground in the standings can cause situations to escalate – especially when the end of the madness, an elusive win, slips away again in the most painful way imaginable. *Never back down*, he thought. He never had, and he wouldn't now. This time, he would take his lumps from any writers who may have heard the confrontation and then he'd seek out Dolan and try to make things right. Maybe tonight, maybe the next morning after they both had a good night's sleep and a chance to cool off. Either way, he'd make the first move. The team was struggling, Dolan was struggling, and Jackson wanted everything to get back to how it had been just a couple weeks earlier. Act like a leader, McGown had said. If the message hadn't been clear before, it was now.

————

Ryan Dolan sat alone atop a table in the trainer's office, frustrated and feeling pathetic. His mind raced from the evening's fireworks, and his crucial errors – both in the game and in the clubhouse – replayed in his head. With his team leading 6-2 in the eighth inning, a ground ball that should have ended the inning instead turned into an errant throw to first, plating two runs. In the fateful thirteenth frame, Dolan booted another routine grounder, which allowed what would have been the game's final out to reach base, setting the stage for the three-run, game-winning blast. Incredibly, it wasn't his worst performance of the season, as that had come just the night before. Perhaps that's what made tonight's mistakes all the more troubling for the sure-handed second baseman: never a star, Dolan could always rely on above-average fielding at several positions to keep him on the big league roster. Every ballplayer goes through twists and turns during the long baseball season, but he felt a sense of dread seeping into his thoughts during the moments between games when he would have benefited from winding down and moving on. What if he was losing his edge? What if this was the new normal for the adequate, though not irreplaceable, ballplayer? Even at his best, Dolan was little more than a seat-filler, keeping the keystone position warm for fast-rising prospect, Mike Brashear. Self-doubt had set up an encampment in the back of his mind and he couldn't shake it loose. In a league that demanded supreme confidence, doubt can spell the end quickly for borderline big leaguers.

Thoughts of the game and his status within it drifted to thoughts of his clubhouse altercation with Tyson Jackson. He let out a sigh and shook his head. That was just stupid, but Jackson should have known better. Or, maybe he should have let the big left fielder speak his piece. No sense overanalyzing what he could no longer control, he thought. That his interaction with Jackson nearly came to blows was the part Dolan regretted. He always had a temper and often struggled with the customary social graces that were second nature to his more outgoing peers, but he also carried a reputation as a good teammate. At least, he tried to be a good teammate. He didn't know Jackson well enough yet – they had only shared a clubhouse for a couple of months and Dolan didn't warm up to new teammates particularly well – but he hoped the two men could settle their differences and leave it in the past.

"Ry, you got a sec?" It was Jackson. "You need time yet or can we bury this?"

"I'm good. I don't know what to say, man – it's been a rough couple of games for me." Dolan hopped to his feet and walked toward Jackson with an outstretched hand, a peace offering. "I'll try to pick my spots better when I need to go off."

"All good, homie. This one's on me. I'm letting these 'L's' get to me too." Jackson paused to consider that maybe now, behind closed doors, he might be able to offer some support to the struggling infielder. "You'd think, being in this game for as long as we have been, these little losing streaks would be easier to brush aside. The pressure builds though, doesn't it?"

"Yeah, it does. I can't get a handle on it. I close my eyes and I just replay my mistakes over and over." Dolan leaned against the wall and crossed his arms. Every time he brought up his struggles, he worried he might be labeled as weak-minded or fragile. That's partly why he lashed out at Jackson in the first place while pouting at his locker. He wanted to be left alone and avoid drawing further attention to himself – avoid leading anyone to believe he was in his own head. No sense showing weakness. Of course, it was too late for that now. He had drawn the wrong kind of attention to himself, and there was no going back. "It just sucks, you know. Everyone is battling and then I'm the jackass who mucks it up for the rest of the guys. It's a shitty feeling, Ty."

"Got to let it go, my man. You've been playing ball a long time – I've seen the back of your baseball card and *I know* this ain't the first time you've struggled." Jackson tried to suppress a sheepish grin while Dolan considered the man's comment. Another jab or just a joke? Maybe, he thought, the high-strung second baseman had been taking himself too seriously all along. Jackson saw his opening to land the punchline when Dolan chuckled and shook his head. "What did you hit as a rookie? .215? Come on my man, what's a couple errors to a light-hitting slap hitter like you?"

Dolan smiled and faked a jab at his teammate, before coming in with a handshake. "Hey, I hit better than you did last year, at least. When was the last time you made contact against a tough righty?"

Maybe this was what he needed after all. The errors and the clubhouse scrum would be a story today, sure. Maybe they'd be the story of the week. But string together a few wins and all would be long forgotten. Water under the bridge.

"That's cold, Ry. Those barbs cut deep." Jackson pulled a big arm around his much smaller teammate and dragged him back toward the clubhouse. "Let's get on with it, huh? Get some sleep, win a game tomorrow."

"Thanks for seeking me out. I'm not a real approach-able guy, but that's a classy, veteran move right there." Dolan spoke from the heart. He didn't want to create any lingering issues in the clubhouse and it felt good to squash it then and there.

"What did you expect? I'm a classy veteran. Only kind of moves I make," Jackson said. "Listen, here's what we're gonna do: we'll get you some extra ground balls, and I'll put in some time catching for you at first. It's just a hiccup, baby. We'll work through it."

The losing streak was tough to shake and hung around for another couple of days – a ninth consecutive loss fol-lowed by an off-day, which was always harder to handle amid the fog of a lengthy cold spell. But eventually, like all losing streaks, it came to an end. The Phillies strung together a few wins, won a few series, and Dolan figured out how to catch and throw again without incident. His confrontation with Jackson, as it turned out, would be the story of the week after all. But that too faded into the background with time and a return to their winning ways. As always, winning cures most ills in the game of baseball.

26

September 1

"Quit looking at your phone, my dude." A slap on the shoulder from teammate Marcus Bergman jostled Mike Brashear from his state of distraction. It was September 1 and while his team was battling deep into the International League's playoffs, Brashear's thoughts were elsewhere, focused on another playoff race in another city. Today, the Philadelphia Phillies would begin to announce a series of call-ups from the depths of their minor league system. The first day of September saw Major League rosters expand from 26 to a maximum of 40 with the arrival of the season's final full month of baseball. Reinforcements often materialize in one of two forms: high-performing veterans with spotty Major League track records or promising prospects earning their first cup of coffee in The Show. Brashear fell squarely in this second group, and while there was little doubt about the big league job that awaited him somewhere down the road, he was uncertain whether his time would come now. Would the Phillies rip a vital piece of Lehigh Valley's postseason hopes from the lineup in order to collect dust on the big league bench? Many within the game believed that developing ballplayers gained valuable experience from being at the center of a playoff run of any kind – even in the minors. On the other hand, perhaps the Phillies would decide that earning an occasional at-bat while watching how big leaguers carried themselves in crunch time was enough of an education to bring him up to the game's highest level? A good argument could be made for both decisions, which was why he sat by himself, fiddled with his phone, and waited for a call he hoped might come.

"I can't help it, man. If it's gonna happen, today's the day. I heard Miguel got the call this morning." Brashear was referring to Miguel Olivarez, a 34-year-old reliever who had pitched brilliantly for the IronPigs, but had only amassed a handful of big league appearances since his first, which came more than a decade ago. He was the definition of what many around baseball refer to as a "Four-A" player: someone with a sparkling minor league stat line who just can't get over the hump in the majors. He was, of course, just the type of guy who tends to get called up in September. After all, everyone needs extra arms in the bullpen by the time September rolls around.

"I hadn't heard that – that's great news for him. Hope he shows them what he can do." Everyone loved Olivarez. Veteran players who some might call big league washouts can choose to detach from their minor league team and mope or view their time in the minors as an opportunity to lead. Olivarez chose the latter every time.

"It's so hard to guess what they might do, you know? And that's the part that kills me." Brashear tossed his phone in his bag and rose with a stretch. "I'm gonna go take a few cuts. Want to hit?"

"Always." Bergman, approaching his twenty-seventh birthday, fell into a different camp than his more widely heralded teammate. While Brashear's future had not been written yet, all signs indicated that the Phillies had a productive, big league-ready second baseman just waiting to be unleashed. Bergman, on the other hand, understood that the door was closing on his own big league hopes. In a few months, as he became, in baseball terms, an "older" prospect, the prospect label would start to fade and he'd be described in some circles as just an older minor leaguer. Someone who might help in a pinch, though certainly not a cornerstone to build around – a useful stopgap, a warm body to round out the edges of a roster in an emergency. He considered it a blessing that he was even in the conversation at all when the big club needed a short-term fill-in to plug a hole in the outfield. The call had never come, but he was always one of two or three names discussed. The way he saw it, it's better to be an older prospect with Major League potential than to be viewed as minor league filler. He worked hard, though, and his dedication didn't go unnoticed. In other words, when Brashear was looking for a partner to put in a few extra swings or hit the gym after hours, he could always count on Marcus Bergman to join him.

"What does your agent say? Any clues about which way they're leaning?" Dogged agents can sometimes extract details of an organization's plans for their clients, especially pertaining to a prized prospect like Brashear. How much he chose to share with his client, however, depended on the agent.

"He just tells me he has a good feeling about it," Brashear said. "He's either trying to stay positive or he knows more than he's letting on."

"Well, that's a good thing, right?"

"I guess so. I just want to know, man. You know what I mean?" Brashear turned to his teammate who gave him a knowing look. Of course, Bergman knew better than most what it was like to wait around for a call-up. It had been years and he still waited. "Put me up there with the game on the line and I'm cool as can be. But this? It's so close, it's right there… and it's driving me crazy."

"They've got a plan for you – you know they do. Take a deep breath, relax. You'll be with the big club before you know it." Bergman was an optimist. After several near misses, he didn't know any other way to carry himself. It got him through the disappointment of falling short so many times before, and he knew that if he dwelled too much on the close calls, it would eat him alive. "It'll happen this season or it'll happen somewhere down the road. Trust me, it *will* happen. And after that, sky's the limit."

"Mikey, can you pop in here for a moment?" The voice of his manager, Victor Cruz, hit Brashear and his body turned to stone. Just up the hallway, his destiny awaited. The logical expectation for the uninitiated was that this would be a joyous conclusion to a season of hard work and studious dedication to fulfilling his immense potential. A league-leading .336 batting average and 39 stolen bases combined with 15 home runs and impressive totals in several other categories would earn most players, especially one as highly touted as Brashear, their first taste of big league action. However, earlier in the week, Cruz had informed Brashear he'd let him know of the Phillies' plans, for better or worse, the moment he heard. Said Cruz, he didn't want his star player distracted by a big league call-up during the playoffs if that call-up wasn't in the cards. It was clear to Brashear that Cruz had received the call. What wasn't clear was whether Brashear had.

"Well, go on, brother! Get in there!" Bergman pushed his teammate toward their manager's door despite Brashear's sudden reluctance. With a final shove, he turned the corner and stood in the doorway, awaiting the team's decision.

"Marcus, come on in. You should hear this too." Bergman, two steps down the hall, pivoted with a skip and joined his teammate beneath the doorframe. Brashear figured bad news would come quickly, and that Cruz might have a little fun with him if his next game would be played in Philadelphia. He was wrong. "Pack your bags. You're going to Philly."

Bergman let out a holler and clapped his teammate on the back. Mike Brashear had graduated to the big leagues, if only for the next month. Come April, however, he would be on everyone's shortlist as an option to start at second base on Opening Day. All he had to do was show he could hang with big league talent for the next month – and he just *knew* he could.

"Congrats, Mikey! Like a rocket ship, my dude. Never look back," Bergman said as he and Brashear embraced. "I'm gonna miss you."

Cruz looked up with a laugh. The surprises weren't over.

"No, Marcus, you won't."

"I'm sorry?" Bergman turned back to his manager with confusion and the slightest hint of panic.

"What part of what I just said is lost on you?" Cruz rose from his desk slowly and walked over to his dependable outfielder – his older prospect – and placed a hand on his shoulder. "Pack your bags, Bergman. You're going to Philly."

Marcus Bergman and Mike Brashear had endured different challenges and expectations throughout their minor league journeys. One rising like a rocket and the other trudging along for years, waiting for an opportunity that he figured might not come. But then for both men, standing in an otherwise unremarkable office inside a minor league ballpark, it did come. While different paths led them to the same moment, they would tackle the next challenge and realize the big league dream together.

27
Three and Twenty-One

Bennett Peterson hadn't entertained thoughts about his next contract since a Spring Training conversation with his manager. At that time, he feared the end of an underwhelming career in baseball, one notable only for its unfulfilled promise, was drawing nearer. Nearly six months later, as he put the finishing touches on his finest season in professional baseball, he had arrived as the dominant late-inning reliever many hoped he might become. And with his success, it was reasonable to think that riches and security would follow close behind. Of course, Peterson knew better than to make assumptions. For a man who had seen more disappointment than most, nothing was a given. The life of a bullpen hand is a transient one; fortunes turn quickly when successes and failures manifest in one-inning increments. A season's worth of shutdown bullpen work should earn him a substantial payday, but he would never count on it before the call came.

And then one day in September, the call came.

"B.P., what's shakin', my man?" The unmistakable voice of Seth Rosenthal brought a smile to Peterson's face. Rosenthal negotiated Peterson's first contract when he was just a pup and had been along for the rollercoaster ride ever since. From year to year, even with a full roster of more reliable, more lucrative clients, he always brought

Peterson a fair deal. Heading into each season, the pitcher half-expected to be playing out the last chance he would get. But then, each offseason would bring a few calls from Rosenthal and one of those calls always led to the next contract. This season, he didn't have to wait until the dead of winter to contemplate his future.

"Just getting a little post-game treatment. A little downtime before the flight to Arizona tonight." Peterson had registered another lockdown inning in the team's 4-2 victory over the visiting Chicago Cubs. More of the same from the lefty who had begun the season as an unknown quantity and would end it as the team's most consistent late-inning option. Could he succeed as a closer? If the Phillies allowed him to reach free agency, he might get that opportunity. Again, he had resisted the temptation of thinking about what tomorrow might bring and he wasn't about to entertain distracting what-ifs at this late stage of the season. Not when his team was engaged in a pennant race few anticipated six months earlier. Not when he was *this close* to rewriting his own narrative.

"I just got off the phone with your GM." Peterson's heart dropped while Rosenthal spoke. "They've made you an offer and it's a good one."

"The suspense is killing me. What did they offer?"

"21 over three." Seven million dollars for each of the next three years. Across the past several seasons, he had hopped between minor league contracts and major league minimums. At 31 years of age, he would see his first million. "It's a solid offer, for sure. It's fair. There is more for you out there, of course."

"What do you mean?" Peterson was still processing what the Phillies' offer meant let alone anything else. The deal was two years longer than any he had signed in his career previously. There were two more zeroes and more than 20-and-a-half million dollars more than he had ever earned. How much more could a left-handed enigma expect? "There's more for me out where?"

"This is a generous offer from Philadelphia, a testament to the team's faith in you – it's good money for what you've accomplished this season. You're my guy. You know that. I think you can earn closer money on the open market." Rosenthal's job was to get his clients the longest and most lucrative deals he could manage. Like any good agent, Rosenthal wanted Peterson to understand what he might be walking away from by accepting the offer from his current team. "At least five teams will need a closer this offseason. We can likely add a year and about three mil annually if you test the market. You'd have the chance to pile up those saves if you wait it out and stay open-minded about signing elsewhere."

"There's risk…"

"Yes, there is risk. There's always risk when you decline twenty-one million dollars." Rosenthal had a good way about him – he paused to give Peterson time to consider his options; he always seemed to know just when to give the big lefty space to think. It was a lot to process for a man lacking experience processing such things. "Look, you have options and that's a good position to be in. After what we've been through together, it feels good to be able to say that, B.P."

"You're not kidding – and I'm grateful, Seth. Truly." Peterson breathed in deeply and considered how far he had come in six months. A desperate man in March, and potentially, a rich man in September. "The question is, how much is enough?"

"The million-dollar question – the *twenty-one* million dollar question, to be precise." Rosenthal laughed. It was a conundrum he had seen time and time again, and the answer depended on the client and his propensity to roll the dice. Peterson had never been much of a gambler. "I don't know, you tell me: how much is enough?"

"We like Philadelphia. As much as a place can feel like home after six months, it's our home." Whether Peterson would accept the Phillies offer was never in question – they wouldn't say it, but both men on the line knew that there was no way Bennett Peterson would be able to walk away from twenty-one million dollars. "McGown took a chance on me when I was coming to the end of the line – mentally, at least. I was in my own head and he helped sort me out. I owe it to him to give him a few more years like this one. Besides, we can make a good life for ourselves with twenty-one million in the bank."

"I should say so." Peterson heard a clap through the phone line. There was always a chance for more, but his agent knew Peterson's decision had been prudent. "Let me call Mark. I'll meet you at the airport in Phoenix and we can sign before you take the field. I'm proud of you, B.P. Congratulations."

"Thanks, Seth. Appreciate you sticking by me all these years." Peterson had an earnest manner of speaking – almost apologetic. As if he hadn't given his agent reason to believe in him. Even after a career-year, the old self-doubts still rattled around in his head now and then.

"You did this. Don't ever forget that," Rosenthal replied. "You earned every penny – I'm just the paper-pusher who gets to tell you about it."

"You've done much more than that and you know it."

"Be that as it may – you put in the work and now you're a rich man. Go call your wife and we'll celebrate tomorrow night in Arizona."

Abigail Peterson tiptoed from her daughter's bedroom just as the phone rattled across the countertop downstairs. She latched the door and bounced down the stairs to find a picture of her husband flashing on the screen of her smartphone.

"Hi, honey. You just missed Julie – I put her down for the night." Abigail poured a glass of wine and settled onto the couch with a sigh. "I watched the game today – you looked good! Wish we could have been there tonight to see you off."

"Thanks, Abby. I felt good. I feel even better now," he said, as a smile creased his bearded cheeks. Project management associated with home renovations prevented the girls from attending the final game of Peterson's homestand. Instead, they would have to say their goodbyes on the phone before another road trip took him away for another week and a half. The time away was hard, made even more so because they couldn't spend the last moments of get-away day together. He wished he could share his news in person, but once the deal was done, it would be broadcasted widely. He'd rather she learned of her good fortune from him rather than the local sports broadcasts. "I have some news that you're going to want to hear."

"What is it, Ben?" He could hear her anxiety bleeding through her calm demeanor. These calls hadn't always been pleasant for the young couple. In fact, they usually weren't. "Is everything alright?"

"Philly made me an offer." He could almost hear her heart skip a beat on the other end of the line.

"What did they offer?"

"Three and 21." Silence on the other end.

"Three and 21... 21 *million*? For three years?!" He laughed as her voice rose before she quieted abruptly. He imagined she was forgetting and then quickly remembering the pixie sleeping just up the stairway.

"Yes, 21 million dollars and it's guaranteed money. Seth is flying out to Arizona and I'll sign it tomorrow." Peterson's eyes welled up in spite of himself. He thought about all the times he had called to let her know he had been released or put on waivers or that he was thinking about hanging it up. And each time, she maintained composure; always supportive, always by his side. "That's it, Abby. We won't have to worry about the next contract for a while. We did it."

"You did it, baby! I'm so proud of you. I'm so proud…"

Peterson said goodnight to his wife, collected a few odds and ends, and ran out to the team bus idling in an empty parking lot outside of the ballpark. Arizona awaited. For a team locked in a tight pennant race, it was another chance to leapfrog the division-leading Mets, who carried a one-and-a-half game lead into their own lengthy road trip. Before too long, the two teams would lock horns again – likely with the division on the line. His future now secure, Peterson couldn't wait for what was to come as the season marched toward its climax and a postseason clincher was well within reach.

28

The Story

Rebecca Stoyanos wasn't a narcissist by any measure, but even she couldn't stop admiring her work. After six long months, dozens of interviews, and just as many revisions, there it was: her feature story on Phillies talented rookie Jose Alvarez gracing the home page of *The Philly Voice*.

Times had changed in journalism. Shrinking newsrooms, declining subscription sales, and rising print costs caused many print news outlets to shutter their doors. Their struggles also gave way to the rise of online-only news sources and one such outlet that rose to prominence in the new age of media was Stoyanos' latest employer. Twenty years earlier, her Alvarez feature might have landed on the back page – prime real estate in the world of sports journalism – and she might have framed it as a trophy of sorts. Now, she'd share her prized professional achievement across myriad social channels and tuck a copy away in her portfolio. It wasn't the same, but it didn't take away from the satisfaction she felt as the fruits of her labor cascaded across her screen.

"Hell of a story, Bex." So enraptured with her work, she didn't see Mark Dorfman approach and it caused her cheeks to redden. Had he noticed her reading and re-reading her own piece? Whatever. Every reporter deserves a moment to enjoy a career-defining feature story. "Haven't seen a piece like that in a good, long while."

"I appreciate that Mark. Very kind of you, though I don't know that it's any more impressive than your series on Peterson." Dorfman's series on the big lefty, spread across six columns, was no less thoughtful and well-researched. Of course, recent events led him to craft an unplanned epilogue to the series, as Peterson's contract extension served as a nice bookend to a heartwarming success story.

"Don't kid yourself – people are going to be talking about that Alvarez piece for a long time." Dorfman was right. Her research of Alvarez took her to his hometown of Santa Clara in Cuba where she spent several days with former teammates and coaches, neighbors, and family members cheering on their local hero from afar. The Alvarez family had a rich tradition in baseball, but no man had entered Major League Baseball with as much promise and potential for greatness as Jose Alvarez. And as he wrapped up his first season, no man had delivered on that promise so quickly. "You put *Philly Voice* on the map with that piece. You watch – people are going to be clamoring for the next feature story by the great Rebecca Stoyanos."

"God, don't even say that." As rewarding as the finished product may be, the process was grueling – especially when one considers the demands of her day job chasing stories all over the U.S. "I'm tired just thinking about it."

"Have you spoken with Jose? Has he seen it yet?"

"He texted me earlier – just 'gracias.' We haven't connected otherwise." Stoyanos closed her browser and turned her attention to the lineup card for that night's game, which had been posted in the press box. "Batting third and playing shortstop. Just like he's done almost every game for the past five months. Plug him in and forget about it."

"Yeah, I'd say he's worked out pretty nicely for the Phils. They've had a few pleasant surprises this season. Talent-wise, I wasn't sure they had enough up and down the roster to be this competitive, this late in the season." Dorfman looked up at the lineup card to review the names: Saunders. Valentín. Alvarez. Taylor. Many of the same names that appeared on Opening Day remaining all these months later. The Phillies weren't just surviving the grind, they were thriving. "And yet, here we are."

By most accounts, some might be quick to call the season a success already. In April, many people in baseball believed that the Phillies were at the tail end of their rebuild and on the upswing after several seasons at the bottom of the league's standings. Improvement was expected, but perhaps not quite to the degree that it had arrived. A recent surge quieted the murmurs of discontentment that came with a late-season swoon. With just a few weeks remained in baseball's marathon season, the Phillies were deadlocked with the New York Mets at the top of the National League East division standings – thanks in large part to the contributions of players like Alvarez and a collection of overachievers that had not yet regressed as some experts predicted. The season even offered something for the fans who might pine for the influx of young talent that often results from falling out of contention, but is less common among contenders. After all, amid the team's winning ways, top prospect Mike Brashear had earned his first look at big league pitching.

"Nice to see Brash get his first crack at the big leagues too, huh?" Dorfman pulled out his laptop next to Stoyanos, who gave him a wry grin as he settled in for the long night ahead.

"Brash? What are you guys, old fraternity bros?" Stoyanos couldn't help herself. Dorfman made himself an easy target of jokes among his peers in the press box, but it was all in good-natured fun. He was a favorite of his fellow Philadelphia beat writers, and a mini-celebrity among his counterparts in other cities when he traveled for road trips. "What time is the kegger?"

"What, that's what they call him. I didn't come up with it." Stoyanos laughed as he tried to explain himself. "Don't give me a hard time."

"I'm just messin', you know I love ya." Stoyanos wrapped her arm around Dorfman's shoulder and pulled him toward her like a big sister might do to her little brother. Like any job, writers cooped up in close quarters don't always get along. Some come and go without a word and others only survive on the beat long enough to learn how to find the clubhouse without getting lost. A few regulars, including Stoyanos and Dorfman, did enjoy the company of one another, and often capped off a long night with postgame drinks, a few laughs, and a chance to commiserate about life on the road – a life that few in the working world could hope to understand. Dorfman's admiration for Stoyanos' work was real and the feeling was mutual. Whether she would ever tell him so, his annual behind-the-scenes features series had inspired her to pursue her piece on Alvarez. Theirs was a mutual respect that made the daily grind more manageable as the season headed toward its end.

"Es bonito. Me encanta." *It's beautiful. I love it.* Alvarez, seated at his locker in the team's clubhouse, read and reread Stoyanos' story on his tablet, quoting the especially poignant sections in broken English to teammate Marcel Valentín, who leaned in with an arm around his young teammate's shoulder. Valentín had been the first to introduce himself to the shell-shocked Cuban on his first day in Philadelphia and had taken him under his wing ever since. It's what made the veteran so valuable to the Phillies even if his role as a platoon player led only to modest contributions on the field. If Alvarez and his more celebrated teammates provided the fireworks at the plate, it was Valentín who served as the glue that kept the clubhouse culture intact.

"Ella hizo bien." *She did well.* Valentín was happy that his teammate had been given a platform to tell his story. Americans were only starting to understand life in Cuba in recent years. The more the Western world understood what Alvarez had come from, his lineage in baseball, and the quality of play across the island nation, the more likely it would be for talented players like himself to get their opportunity in Major League Baseball. "Tu mamá estará orgullosa de su bebe." *Your mama will be proud of her baby boy.*

"Sí. Sí, sí, sí." Alvarez set his tablet down and wiped moisture from his eyes. His mother and extended family were arriving from Cuba, finally, in a few days. It would be the first time she stepped foot on U.S. soil and, importantly, the first time she would see her son suit up for the Phillies. She had watched every game he played in Santa Clara, of course, but it was different here. Even he had to pinch himself the moment he first stepped inside the batter's box in front of the raucous South Philly crowd. Now, the stakes were even higher as the team headed toward game #162 locked in a fierce battle for a postseason berth. He could only hope his family had the chance to watch their prodigal son celebrate a clincher on the big league stage before the season's final days.

29

#162

"It's poetic, in a way, that after this long season – what started with pitchers and catchers reporting to Spring Training in February – after the long summer, the highs and lows we all experience at one time or another every year... it all comes down to this. Game 162." An entire region soaked in every word as Leonard Pries described the scene for listeners as only he could. Pries and his broadcast partner Henry Lorenzo had been in the booth long enough to have narrated both the worst of times and the best. Nights like this, with a division title hanging in the balance, ranked right up among the finer moments they'd shared in the broadcast booth.

"Game 162 – I'm ready and I'll tell you what, Leo, these fans are ready!" Lorenzo, the color man, was the voice of the fans. If Pries played it straight, fans could always count his excitable broadcast partner to voice the fans' displeasure at times, and, at moments like this, their joy.

"A packed house tonight, Henry. More than 44,000 waving towels and praying to the Baseball Gods that this is the night that they can say 'I was there' when the Philadelphia Phillies captured their twelfth National League East Division title." Pries and Lorenzo enjoyed such natural chemistry that their commentary always tied together so nicely for listeners across the region. "We're just about underway here in South Philadelphia. It'll be Aaron Tanner on the mound for the Phillies, in search of his seventeenth win, against Juan Acencio of the New York Mets. These two teams have battled all season. They head into tonight's game deadlocked atop the NL East, and it comes down to this: win, clinch the division, and it's a date with the defending champion Los Angeles Dodgers in the Divisional Series. Lose, and it's an offseason of regrets and what-ifs."

"We don't know how this game will unfold, but I can guarantee you this: no one in that clubhouse is thinking about anything other than winning tonight's ballgame and taking this wild ride to Los Angeles. McGown has this team focused on one thing and one thing only, and that's beating the New York Mets here tonight." The urgency in Lorenzo's voice spoke volumes. No one wanted the magic to end – not now, not with the team one win away from bringing postseason baseball back to Philadelphia. A win tonight would assure the Phillies at least a few cracks at the Dodgers and as history informs us, anything can happen in a five-game series. For now, they'd take it one game at a time. After all, that's all they had left.

"We're underway in Philadelphia – it's the Philadelphia Phillies and the New York Mets, tied for the division lead," Pries said to the millions of fans listening at home, hanging on his every word as he set the stage for the final game of the regular season. "Tonight's matchup has a little bit of everything: playoff implications, two talented lineups, and two of the finest young starting pitchers in the game squaring off with everything on the line."

Pries looked to his broadcast partner with a smile and patted him on the shoulder. Decades together in the booth and these moments never got stale.

"First pitch from Tanner is a fastball on the outside corner for strike one, and we're underway at 7:06 in the evening."

The first act in the final chapter of the regular season had begun.

Tanner lived for these moments. The young ace had fallen a bit short of the lofty expectations he had set for himself at the beginning of the season, but under the spotlight of October baseball, he was at his best and there was nowhere else he'd rather be. Through six innings against the high-octane New York Mets offense, he had thrown just 57 pitches and limited the damage to a single in the third inning. No walks, nine strikeouts. An ace performance. After six full, however, the outcome remained in question. Acencio had shown near-equal mastery of the Phillies lineup until it broke through with a run in the sixth. Would it be enough? The way Tanner was pitching, it just might.

"How are you feeling?" McGown leaned toward his starter as the two stood at the top of the dugout stairs in the bottom of the seventh.

"Great. Barely breaking a sweat." It wasn't too much of an exaggeration either. In an era notable for the careful management of pitcher innings and pitch counts, Tanner was making life easy for his coaches. At this rate, it was reasonable to think Tanner might go the distance. "This crowd..."

Tanner scanned the upper reaches of the second and third decks and got lost in the bedlam. A sellout, the team's sixty-third in a row, was on fire when the first pitch was thrown and had come unglued after the Phillies plated the only run of the game. The City of Brotherly Love held a reputation for passionate fandom. That passion sometimes made life difficult for players in a city that rewarded hard work and hustle and blackballed anyone who might lack those traits. Fail to bust it down the first base line on a ground ball? Choose to slow down instead of diving for a ball? Good luck getting the fanbase back on your side. Uniforms are meant to be dirty. In Philadelphia, show the fans you give a damn with it all on the line and they're yours forever. Tonight, a max-effort playing environment where everyone up and down the roster was giving their all, was one of those nights. Especially for a young man named Aaron Tanner.

Sometimes, however, max effort isn't enough. On a difficult play in the top of the eighth inning sure-handed defender Marcel Valentín ranged toward the second base bag and, in an act of desperation, came up with the ball at the tip of his glove after an all-out dive across the infield dirt. Had he given anything less than his best effort, it would have been a surefire, leadoff single and no one would have thought twice. Instead, he came up with the ball, hopped to his feet, and rushed the throw. The ball soared over a leaping Barrett Taylor at first base, landed in the Mets dugout, and allowed the runner to scamper to second base. After a sacrifice bunt moved the runner to third, a deep sacrifice fly to left field knotted the game at one apiece. Momentum, a fickle beast, had switched uniforms.

In the most important game of his life, Tanner completed nine innings and, on account of his economical use of pitches – 89 in total – left his manager with an unorthodox decision to make.

"How's the arm?"

"I can pitch all night." The manager didn't expect to hear anything less from his starter, a tireless bulldog who seldom offered a hint of when he might need a rest. Of course, you can't always take a player's self-assessment as gospel. McGown, however, had been in the game long enough to recognize the signs of a pitcher wearing down. After nine innings, Tanner remained as sharp as a tack.

"Okay. I'll keep rolling you out there, then."

That's all that needed to be said. No Phillies starting pitcher had seen the tenth inning since former star Cliff Lee went 10 full on a cool April night in San Francisco in 2012. The Giants topped the Phillies in eleven innings that night and Lee earned a no-decision for his troubles. Tanner was hoping for a better outcome; he wanted so desperately to be at the bottom of the dog-pile when his team recorded the game's final out and the Phillies clinched a division title as improbable in October as it had been in April. They'd have to drag him off the field to get him out of the game. He hoped it wouldn't have to come to that.

———

"What an unprecedented display of faith McGown has shown in his ace, Aaron Tanner." Pries, a product of another era, beamed like a proud parent as the Phillies' starter completed his tenth inning. When he first broke into the league, it wasn't unfathomable that a pitcher might toss 10 or more innings if he was rolling. The game had changed, of course, and Tanner's was a feat unheard of in recent times. "And this young man, in his twenty-sixth year, has rewarded his manager's confidence with another 1-2-3 inning. Henry, this game will surely be remembered among the all-timers in this city, whatever the outcome."

"Absolutely. What grit from that young man right there. He has elevated his game to the highest possible level at the most critical time."

"In the bottom of the tenth, it'll be Valentín and then the heart of the order: Alvarez, Taylor, and Valencia."

Pries waited for the commercial break before addressing Lorenzo. "What do you think, Henry? A chance for atonement for Valentín?"

"Wouldn't that be picture perfect?" Lorenzo turned his eyes to the on-deck circle as Valentín took a few swings. "I'd sure like to see it."

When, on this night the final out was recorded, however it happened, Valentín would be able to reflect on his season with pride. Never a crucial piece of any roster from the time he broke into the league right up to his fight to make the Phillies roster in the spring, his eleventh big league season had been one to remember. Valentín set career highs in every category and, even as part of a platoon at second base, had been in the conversation as a Gold Glove Award candidate, which was given each season in recognition of the league's best fielders. His defense was *that* good, and it only made his errant throw even more surprising. It also may have made his final at-bat that much sweeter.

"Two and one the count to Valentín. And the pitch... swing and a liner into center, falling fast! It's going to drop in for a base hit! Valentín is aboard with a lead-off single."

A wave of euphoria swept over 44,000 delirious fans and fell upon the first base bag, where a jubilant, vindicated Valentín leaped into the air with a fist pump. His teammates jumped in place in the dugout, many standing on the top step or holding onto the railing that ran parallel to the foul line. Each man was ready to launch himself onto the field the moment Valentín crossed home plate – if he crossed home plate.

Valentín's base hit brought Alvarez to the plate with the chance to be a hero – a hero to the capacity crowd, and to his extended family seated in their own box above home plate. A moment so many children dreamed about on the sandlots across Cuba was now unfolding in real life for the talented shortstop coming to the plate for the final at-bat of his first major league season. Alvarez dug his cleats into the dirt and let the noise of the crowd wash over him. Cubans loved their baseball, but he had never experienced anything quite like this before. Adrenaline, like an electric current, coursed through his body as he readied for the first pitch, which he hoped would be the game's last pitch. The ball approached, and he unfurled a wild, looping swing and a miss. It was an uncharacteristic display for the man with the prototypical swing that had been the talk of the league all season long. Compact, quick, and packed with power. *The next swing would be different*, he thought. And it was.

"Nothing and one the count to Alvarez. Valentín a few steps off the first base bag here in the tenth inning of game 162." Pries reset the scene for listeners as if anyone had been listening with anything less than their full attention. On the contrary, the entire region hung on every pitch. "He comes set, and the pitch... swing and long drive! Deep left field! It's long gone, and the Philadelphia Phillies are your National League East Division Champions!"

Lorenzo laughed and pounded on the broadcaster's desk like a drum. The kid inside had burst through and amid the euphoria, he didn't much care if he came across as a fan first, then a broadcaster. In the moment, that's very much what he was. Pries, filled with joy himself, would not be distracted from capturing the moment for his audience across the region. "Alvarez is mobbed at home plate and this crowd is going crazy! Fireworks fill the air on a most beautiful fall night in Philadelphia. They'll celebrate tonight and then board a plane for LAX, as a date with the Dodgers, the defending champions, awaits."

"Los Angeles, here we come!" Lorenzo yelled out over the noise of the crowd and fireworks exploding high above South Philly. "Unbelievable! Jose took that one wild swing, something we hadn't seen all year, but he followed it up with the perfect swing and the perfect moment for this ball club. Have yourself a night, Jose Alvarez!"

"Indeed, it was the perfect swing on a pitch that caught a little too much of the plate, and he made him pay."

Alvarez tossed his arms up to protect himself from the pounding of his rabid teammates, though his half-hearted defense was of little use. The sound inside his helmet rumbled like a thunderclap while pairs of hands tossed him back and forth like a rag doll. In one motion, 26 grown men hopped up and down as if each had been transported to their childhood, bouncing on a trampoline without a care in the world. Few moments in pro ball rustle up the kid inside quite like a division-clinching walk-off winner.

Amid the celebration, tapering off only slightly as Alvarez' teammates considered relocating to the club-house for the party's champagne-soaked second act, he peered toward the boxes behind home plate in search of family. Like ducklings following their mother toward the water, a dozen or more brothers, sisters, cousins, and aunts and uncles streamed down stadium steps toward the field, following the family's matriarch, Alvarez' mother. He ran to the first base line to greet them with hugs and kisses. This was a moment he had fantasized about on the sandlots and back alleys in his native Santa Clara, Cuba. As he drew his mother closer – and drew the season to an end – he hoped there would be a few more childhood dreams in their future.

30

Baseball's Second Season

More than a decade had passed since the Philadelphia Phillies last won baseball's ultimate prize. That time, a period of good fortune driven by homegrown talent that netted five consecutive division titles and a world championship, grew from humble beginnings. The team that snapped a 13-year postseason drought in 2007 entered baseball's second season with a "just happy to be here" mentality and was promptly dispatched in three quick games against the more seasoned Colorado Rockies. That, of course, is a common outcome for Cinderella stories that emerge as contenders a year or two ahead of schedule. Wide-eyed and awestruck, it's easy to get caught up in the moment and find yourself on the golf course before you have time to blink. Sometimes, however, there's benefit to being cast as the upstart, playing without the burden of expectations. In 2011, the Phillies won 102 games and coasted into the playoffs with a "World title or bust" mentality. The real challenge, experts said at the time, would come in the World Series. Of course, that wasn't the case at all: the St. Louis Cardinals dispatched the Phillies in the Divisional Series before the team could settle in for a meaningful postseason run. Many years earlier, another powerhouse, the Seattle Mariners, won a record 116 regular season games, only to fall short, losing to the New York Yankees in the American League Championship Series. Indeed, baseball history is littered with similar tales of regular season domination followed by postseason disappointment.

Expectations can weigh heavy on the broad shoulders of baseball's biggest superstars. On the other end of the spectrum, no one expected the 2013 Boston Red Sox to win the World Series, but they did. No one expected much from the 83-win Cardinals in 2006, but they won just enough games to get into the tournament and, once there, just enough to win the whole thing. When you're playing with house money, crazy things can happen. Underdogs have tried to describe the mentality in many ways, often falling back on naïveté to explain how they overcame the odds to rise as champions. "We didn't know any better" or "we were just dumb enough to think we had a chance" are common refrains. Whatever the case may be, baseball is a game of instincts and reflexes. Mountainous expectations lead to nerves and tightness. Playing tight leads to mistakes, and mistakes lead to losses. As the Phillies deplaned at Los Angeles International, days away from Game One of the best-of-five Divisional playoff round against the heavily favored Dodgers, they were as loose as could be.

Bennett Peterson lumbered down the steel stairs on the jetway toward the bus that would escort the ball club to their accommodations at the Beverly Hills Four Seasons Hotel. He wore the same suit he had worn upon his arrival in every new city since April. He only owned two suits anyway, so if this one hadn't worn out yet, why change things now? Plus, it was his most stylish option – a gift from his wife after he made the Opening Day roster, and after she had learned of the team's road trip dress policy.

"You ever bring that thing to the dry cleaners?" Raul Valencia, Peterson's much more fashionable teammate, asked as they climbed aboard the bus. "I guess a better question is… do you know that you can't machine-wash a suit?"

Peterson scratched his beard and surveyed his suit before cracking a smile. He thought he looked pretty good.

"My lady takes good care of me," he replied. True enough, Abigail Peterson always had her husband's suit clean and ready to wear before every road trip. Like many of his teammates, she wasn't sure what he might wear if she didn't look after him. After all, she hadn't married him for his fashion sense. "I'm thinking about starting my own line of suits for big fellas, what do you think?"

"Built-in tuxedo T-shirts?"

"Of course." The thought of Peterson selling a line of suits was hilarious to anyone who knew the man, and his deadpan delivery only made the joke better. These lighter moments, in between the last big game and the next, kept the team loose as it embarked on its unlikely playoff run. Few expected the Phillies to beat the mighty Dodgers, a task made more difficult by playing the first two games on the road. But then, it never really mattered to Philadelphia – the team or its host city – what other people thought. Right or wrong, they liked their chances. They always did.

"Same lineup?" Paul Cartwright, the Phillies bench coach, sat with his manager in an empty clubhouse beneath Dodger Stadium. A buzz of energy surrounded the old ballpark like a blanket, but here in the tunnels deep underground, no noise seeped through in the early morning hours before Game One of the Divisional Series.

"Same lineup." After months of fiddling with the order, John McGown had grown comfortable with a specific mix by the time July rolled around. Save for a couple of effective platoons, he seldom strayed from what had worked so well for much of the season. Saunders leading off, one half of his second base platoon batting second (Dolan tonight), followed by Alvarez, his electric impact player, sitting in the three-hole. To varying degrees, the players in the top third of his lineup offered a blend of speed, contact, and apart from Dolan, power. The second third was just as easy to write out: Taylor, Valencia, and Jackson. Power, more power, and the "professional hitter" acquired midseason to shore up the team's left field platoon.

"Who's catching? Toperick?"

"Yep." Rick Toperick had blossomed as one of the best receivers in the National League, though his bat left plenty of room for improvement. In the eighth position, the Phillies would put up with the light-hitting catcher's nominal contributions to the offense in order to keep his cannon arm and flawless game-calling abilities in the lineup. He'd hit just behind the club's right fielder, Jayson Warren.

"Best receiver in the game if you ask me." Cartwright, a former catcher, held a deep appreciation for anyone capable of such mastery of the game's most physically demanding and mentally exhausting position. "You know from the first pitch that he's going to call a hell of a game."

"That's the plan." McGown finished his lineup card and pinned it to the clubhouse wall. On a whiteboard, he wrote out the day's schedule for meetings and batting practice. The energy surrounding the game would be unwieldy, so McGown felt it was important to ensure the team's pregame routine remained as intact as possible. Baseball players are creatures of habit and the same discipline that placed them among the top one percent of athletes in pro ball was, for most, a reflection of the diligence by which they kept to their schedules. Aside from the team-mandated responsibilities McGown committed to the whiteboard – full squad stretch at 3:45, batting practice at 5:00 – each player had their pregame rituals timed down to the minute. Those schedules varied from player to player, but the field before a game was always buzzing with activity of some sort, and it was clear to anyone watching closely enough who wasn't quite on schedule. The ballplayer running a few minutes behind always looked a bit more frantic than everyone else, attitude a bit surlier, movements a bit rushed. A few minutes off and nothing was quite right.

"Morning, Skipper." McGown's own routine was interrupted by an early arrival in the form of Rick Toperick.

"You're here early. Video?" Ever a student of the game, Toperick was often the first to arrive in order to log some extra preparation time ahead of a new series.

"Some. Corino wants to show me some heat maps." The injection of data into game day preparation was a new twist for an old-timer like McGown. He admired the data analysts that the team employed, like Alex Corino, and appreciated their growing impact on the game. Together, it all helped improve the product on the field and McGown recognized that the Phillies' front office philosophies translated to the team's improvement in the standings. "You know I love a pretty heat map."

"What I like is what you do with the information." McGown and Cartwright shook their catcher's hand as they walked by. "That's why you're in the lineup tonight."

"Sure as hell won't be because of my bat," Toperick quipped, well aware and at peace with his greatest deficiency. He understood his role and appreciated what kept him tethered to the big league roster for going on five years. "But if I can help prevent runs…"

"Best game manager in baseball – that's why we keep running your ass out there." Cartwright never missed an opportunity to praise his favorite catcher. He had been equally inept in the batter's box during his playing days, though not half as good behind it when compared to Toperick's defensive skills. "We don't need a whole lot of offense in the eight-hole."

Toperick retreated to a suite where Corino waited with a stack of papers. Blessed with a photographic memory, the steady catcher would commit the contents of each sheet – grids of data points, spray charts, and heat maps exposing the tendencies of each Dodgers hitter – during the next few hours. By the time his pitching staff arrived around 2:30 in the afternoon, he would be ready to walk the relief corps and that evening's starter, reliable veteran Jimmy Moore, through the game plan. In an era of advanced metrics, at a time when the league's advancements in analytics made it possible to measure just about everything, Toperick's performance graded out at the top of the league in several popular categories. There was one area, however, that McGown always focused on that was often overlooked by the rest of the league: how often his pitchers shook off one of the catcher's pitch calls. It rarely happened. In other words, McGown's pitching staff trusted their catcher and that, above all else, mattered most to his manager.

31

The Best of Times

Preston Saunders stood on the mound and soaked in the bedlam unfolding on the field in front of him. Champagne streamed down his face and it stung his eyes, but never touched his lips. This was a moment he wanted to savor – to commit every detail to memory forever. His teammates, soaked with the content of several bottles of champagne that they had commandeered from the clubhouse, hung tight to the warning track dirt along the baselines while thousands of screaming fans pressed up against the edge of the dugout to celebrate alongside the unlikely victors. Hidden beneath the stadium, a clubhouse encased in protective tarps stood empty and silent. Soon enough, the party would migrate inside. For now, however, the Philadelphia Phillies felt an obligation to celebrate right alongside its rabid fan base. More than 44,000 fans had filled the ballpark and now, 45 minutes after the team had dispatched the defending champs, most remained. Game four, the final game of the National League Divisional Series, was over. By a count of three games to one, the Phillies had beaten the heavily favored Dodgers and were advancing to the next round. One final stop before a World Series berth. Only the St. Louis Cardinals stood in their way.

"Is it like you thought it would be?" Rick Toperick met Saunders on the mound and pulled him in with an embrace.

"Better."

"Nothing quite like it." While most professional athletes enjoy a taste of what Saunders and Toperick soaked in from their perch atop the mound at some point in their minor league or amateur career, the sturdy catcher had never been so fortunate. "I'd like to do this a couple more times."

"You're telling me," Saunders replied as he kicked the loose dirt at his feet. "Four more wins versus the Cards and we'll be right here again. Four more after that..."

He trailed off and both men stood in silence, the chill of the cool October air settling into their champagne-soaked uniforms. Mist from the spray of popping bottles cascaded from the edge of the field into the first few rows of a delirious crowd while noise filled the air above South Philly. Saunders and Toperick jogged off the mound toward the dugout, and a roar from the crowd announced their arrival. History would remember both men fondly for their postseason heroics and an entire region hoped their performance against the Dodgers was just the beginning. That Saunders helped lift his team to its first postseason series win since 2010 wasn't surprising. After all, he was one of the game's young stars, a true five-tool player blossoming into a spark plug at the top of the Phillies' lineup and a leader in the clubhouse. Few would have predicted Toperick's impact, however.

During the short series with Los Angeles, Toperick's ability to call a good game behind the plate was less surprising than his power stroke at the dish. In four starts, the catcher matched his season total with four home runs while knocking in seven runs from the eighth position in the batting order. He hit .563 in the series, and if the league recognized a Most Valuable Player in its Divisional Series round, he surely would have collected some hardware. As it was, Toperick's breakout was no less memorable and would live on in the memories of the Phillies faithful for years to come. A few more wins and who knows? He might still collect some hardware when all was said and done.

Sing-song chants of "Let's go, Philly!" and "Thank you, Phillies!" rained down on the team as they filed past the dugout and down the long tunnel leading to the clubhouse. Celebrating with their fans was a thrilling continuation of the on-field dog-pile that began with an embrace between pitcher and catcher, Bennett Peterson and Toperick, respectively, a few feet in front of the mound. It was an unforgettable undercard to a main event that was about to begin. The dark echo chamber that connects the dugout to the clubhouse rattled with the same lyrics that the fans had chanted in the stands. Twenty-five grown men hooted and hollered like Little League kids while their families and a swarm of reporters and team personnel awaited their arrival. The giddy reaction fit the moment like a glove; it is a children's game, after all.

Jose Alvarez, the energetic Cuban dynamo, was the first to reach the clubhouse and let out a holler to announce the team's arrival into the tarp-covered clubhouse. Peterson lifted his wife Abigail into the air and spun her like a carousel while a sports anchor from the local news tried to inch his way closer, microphone in hand, on the hunt for a quick sound bite. Aaron Tanner, owner of two of the team's three victories over the defending champs, kissed his wife and pulled her close in a more subdued manner. Filled with joy, he knew there was still work to be done before the team allowed itself to celebrate too much. At 11:30 p.m. on a Thursday night in Philadelphia, Tanner's mind had already drifted toward his next start, which would be the second game of the next round. It promised to be the biggest of his career, surpassing the Divisional Series clincher. And as predictable as the sun rising and setting, it would soon be surpassed by his next start. Each performance grew more and more important as the team moved closer to its goal.

"Aaron, a word?" Tom Flanagan of the *Philadelphia Inquirer* stepped forward with pad and pen. Tanner smiled. He always liked the *Inquirer*'s longtime beat writer.

"Anything for my favorite reporter." A shout of "hey!" rose above the music and cheers. Rebecca Stoyanos took issue with Tanner's comment, but only in jest.

"Can you give me a sense of how you're feeling right now? Has it sunk in yet?"

"I can't even explain it. Anytime I walk out to the mound, I expect to win – not once did I think of us as underdogs. I..." Tanner paused while affixing goggles over his head as quickly as he could manage. "You'll have to excuse me for a moment, Tom."

Marcel Valentín and Tyson Jackson stood behind him with a bottle of champagne in each hand. Before he could react, Flanagan, along with Tanner, his wife, and everyone within range, was soaked. The interview was over. These moments, joyous for the players and their loved ones, presented the men and women of the team's press corps with a few unavoidable occupational hazards. Most took their inevitable champagne baths in stride and did the best they could with repetitive quotes from distracted ballplayers. For the veteran writers covering the postgame celebration, it came with the territory.

The road ahead remained a long one for the Phillies and everyone associated with the ball club. For now, however, as the press departed and the real party began, everyone in the clubhouse pressed pause on the future to enjoy the outcome of months of hard work. Hugs and high-fives all around; it was a good night to be alive in South Philly.

32

The Aftermath

John McGown sat in his office, swirling the contents of an Old Fashioned, a simple whiskey drink, around a large, square ice cube. He watched the brown liquid climb up the sides of the glass as if it was trying to escape. Raising the glass to his lips, McGown paused to examine its contents while Mark Johnson, the Phillies GM and resident mixologist, looked on from across the desk.

"It's perfect." McGown took a sip. His first taste of an adult beverage since early February. "Superb."

This ritual, shared between the team's field general and its roster architect, was an annual tradition that closed out each of their previous seasons together, and ushered in a new offseason filled with the promise of improvement and the hindsight to analyze missteps. The date was November 6 and the baseball season was over. The marathon had ended and little by little, the world would turn its attention away from baseball and on to other area sports. Confetti still clung to the streets and team colors flew proudly, though not in the City of Brotherly Love. Somewhere to the West, Cardinals fans entered the offseason with yet another World Championship in tow, having dispatched the best that the American League had to offer, the cross-state Kansas City Royals, in six games. The

Phillies? Bounced by the eventual champs in the League Championship Series, also in six games.

"It was a good season," Johnson said while McGown continued to study and savor his cocktail. "You should be proud of what the team accomplished."

"I am."

"I think the pieces are in place for a sustained run, I really do." Johnson walked across the room and grabbed a glass for himself. "We made it much further than most had predicted. Next year, we'll go further still."

"I have no doubt we will."

Indeed, an extended run of competitive baseball was a realistic goal for the Phillies. The playoff contender that fans and reporters had predicted might manifest a couple of seasons down the road had arrived early. Under McGown's tutelage, players like Jose Alvarez burst onto the scene and delivered as advertised. Other less-heralded players like lefty flamethrower Bennett Peterson and solid citizen Marcel Valentín, expected to live on the edges of the big league roster, instead played pivotal roles on a division-winning ball club. Best-laid plans seldom work out as well as they had for Philadelphia, and the team's success had some around the league wondering if they simply caught lightning in a bottle for one special season. Of course, Johnson and McGown wanted to believe that there was more to it than that. Contending deep into October qualified as a success, but both men hoped the next season would bring more.

Decisions awaited in the weeks and months to come, but for now, the mood was one of reflection. Together, McGown and Johnson would reflect on the good and the bad, the surprises and the shortfalls. The team had arrived, sure enough. Heading into a new season, unexpected success would breed heightened expectations. Not quite that "World Series or bust" mentality of 2011, but shortcomings would be met with less patience than the team enjoyed the previous season.

"We have a few arbitration cases coming up," Johnson said. Arbitration was an annual business tradition in baseball that few participants enjoyed: the team and player exchange salary figures and if an agreement can't be made before a certain date on a figure that satisfies both parties, they meet to debate the merits and failings of said player and the process can become contentious. Most players and teams settled on a salary figure somewhere in the middle to avoid the hearing. Sometimes, however, they don't. "Saunders. Valencia. He'll be a tough one."

"Tough how?" McGown didn't see it. Raul Valencia had taken a major step during the past season at the plate and in the field. He was a reliable bat in the middle of the lineup and the fielding – never a strength – was improving. "He's a good player. He's an important part of this ball club and he should be paid like one."

"The defense is a question mark and it impacts his value." Johnson, more than McGown, was inclined to consider a player's history more closely than the incremental improvements of recent times when it came to arbitration. Was the improvement sustainable? Would it continue? Was Valencia due for a step back? These were all questions to consider when the conversation involved millions of dollars. "The question is whether his agent understands that, or will he choose to ignore half of the game? Certainly, they won't emphasize areas that need improvement. That's the concern."

"The defense is improving." McGown took a sip of his drink and cleared his throat. "He's a rising star and he'll only get better. Pay the man."

"I don't think it'll get to arbitration. I'd like to think we can settle on fair value," Johnson replied, partly to put his manager's mind at ease. He had no intention of ripping the man's roster apart. Arbitration simply presented more hurdles, more heartburn, than the typical contract negotiation. "I just hope he's as pragmatic as he seems."

"He's a smart kid. He knows he still has a long way to go to be the player he wants to be." If anything, Valencia was harder on himself than anyone else. When the team moved him to third base, he wanted to be the best third baseman he could be. When it didn't come naturally, it ate him alive. Practice helped. So did a season with a batting line highlighted by 30 home runs and 105 runs batted in. "I don't think you have to worry about Raul Valencia overstating his value."

"As far as Saunders goes –" Johnson was interrupted by McGown, respectfully, before he could finish. The old man didn't want to hear the words Preston Saunders and arbitration.

"Lock him up. Pay him what he's worth. Pay him more than he's worth." Saunders was a star – the centerpiece of the team's roster. McGown saw no reason to go year-to-year with one of the league's most gifted athletes.

"We're exchanging figures with his agent on a long-term deal and I'm hopeful he wants to commit to us as much as we want to commit to him." Johnson slid a sheet of paper across the desk to McGown. Scribbled on the sheet were the numbers seven and one hundred and twenty-four. A strong show of commitment to an otherworldly talent.

"Good."

"It's a big contract and I think it shows him that we are committed." Johnson tucked the sheet back in his pocket and looked through the window on the empty playing field below, glowing beneath the stadium lights. "And it shows this city that we're not afraid to invest in our future."

The two men sat together until darkness fell heavy on the ballpark and winter's chill materialized in the first snowflakes of the offseason. If the regular season put McGown and his players front and center in the conscious-ness of the Philadelphia fan base, the winter months, often referred to as the Hot Stove League, gave Johnson a turn in the spotlight. If any of the team's fans weren't familiar with the team's general manager, they soon would be.

"I'll tell you what I'd like – if you're taking requests." McGown rose to join his contemporary at a window over-looking the field, now coated with a light dusting of snow. Some general managers didn't welcome input, but Johnson was different. He viewed his relationship with McGown as a critical part of the team's success – the intangible, unquantifiable element of a winning formula.

"I'm all ears, always."

"Get me another Aaron Tanner. Get me two of 'em," McGown said. "When I looked across the diamond at the Cardinals bench, that's the one thing that stood out to me. Game after game, they just throw one ace after another at you. Relentless."

"I'll do my best," Johnson replied. McGown was quite certain the perceptive GM would have come upon a sim-ilar observation when comparing rosters with the team's League Championship Series adversary.

"Would have been nice to win that series." McGown brought the conversation back to the site of the Phillies' biggest disappointment during a season that had few. "Can you even imagine how this city would have reacted? I think we might have pasted Kansas City."

"We matched up pretty well with them," Johnson said in agreement. "St. Louis, not so much."

The Phillies had given the eventual World Champions a solid fight before the magic ran out in downtown St. Louis. There was no notable regression, no single player exposed on the biggest stage before the World Series. Rather, the team always seemed to come up just short of swinging momentum in their favor. Instead of a two-run double, it was an inning-ending pop up. Instead of a go-ahead home run, a strikeout. A team noted for its propensity to deliver in the biggest spots, the Phillies wasted several such opportunities against a more experienced, focused Cardinals team. Perhaps that's the way it was always meant to go. There's no shame in losing to a talented, veteran-laden team like the St. Louis Cardinals.

"I told the guys, an at-bat here or there, and that series could have gone the other way. They get it, though. They're proud of what we accomplished." McGown stood to stretch, signifying closing time. Or at least, last call. "The taste only made them hungrier. If everyone stays healthy and does their job, I sure would like to get another crack at St. Louis again next October."

"We just might," Johnson replied. "We just might."

Johnson and McGown were headed in different directions – both literally and figuratively. McGown's job was done and, aside from the occasional charity event or press conference to announce free agent signings, he wouldn't see much of Johnson until pitchers and catchers reported to Spring Training the following February. Johnson, on the other hand, would continue to make the ballpark his second home through the long winter. Through rain and snow, at all hours of the day and night, the general manager's office was sure to be bathed in light within an otherwise quiet stadium. He looked forward to the occasional escape – a trip to Florida for the annual Winter Meetings with other league GM's, visits with potential free agent signings in warmer climates. But even the long days and nights at the ballpark, surrounded by a skeleton crew of front office personnel, weren't all that bad. He loved his job and he loved his team. For the next few months, he'd try to patch a few holes and, if the financials made sense, make a few splashes. Baseball offered no guarantees, but he'd do his best to give McGown a fighting chance. A few shrewd signings and a little luck along the way, they hoped, might be the recipe to conjure another deep run and another shot at the World Championship the team, its city, and its fans all craved.

33

The End Is a Beginning

"Can we watch it again? *Please?*" Ella stared at her father's face and leaned in until her big blue eyes were inches from his own. "I want to watch it again."

"Sure, baby bear. We can watch it again." Aaron Tanner had been home for more than a month now and relished the chance to live the life of stay-at-home dad after eight months on the road. The nomadic life of the big league ballplayer provides plenty of downtime in interesting cities and elegant hotel rooms, but little time for the quiet moments with family that he missed so very much. Lazy Saturday mornings curled up with a toddler and his loving wife offered fleeting glimpses of what life might be like if he had a regular job. Life on the road was hard, so Tanner tried to be present for the quiet moments at home enjoying the dad life to make up for it to a degree.

It was early December and the baseball player that lived inside the Phillies ace was stirring to life. After a full month off, aside from routine workouts to maintain the faintest notion of physical fitness, December 1 brought with it the first day of his offseason throwing program. Tanner had 10 weeks to prepare his arm for the rigors of Spring Training and then, following that, another long baseball season. Ten weeks to build on a solid season, ten weeks to prepare for the next step in his career progression and, hopefully, another postseason run.

Preparations would have to wait, however. During the morning hours, with the faint light of a mid-winter sunrise peeking through their windows, Tanner was content to stay under the covers with his family while the magic of Disney unfurled itself on their television. The foundation of strong and consistent performance during the regular season began with meticulous preparations in the offseason months. The foundation of a strong marriage and family life also settled its roots during the quiet time between the previous season's final pitch and the first long toss of Spring Training. Tanner, ever a student of the game, understood the value of balance and remained committed to maintaining a healthy family life along with the rigors and pressures that come with a career in pro ball.

"More coffee?"

"Only if you're getting up, hon." Jessica Tanner reached across the toddler nestled between her and her husband and squeezed his hand. "I'll never say no to a cup of coffee."

He kissed her on the forehead and pulled away, despite pleas from his daughter to stay. It's tough for a four-year-old to understand the demands of a professional baseball career, particularly its stranglehold on her father's time. Today, daddy made it clear that he planned to return in a few minutes with a hot cup of coffee in-hand. Tomorrow, for all she knew, he might be gone for weeks. When they had fallen in love, Jessica and Aaron understood what they were signing up for. Time apart, peculiar hours, and an extraordinary amount of travel. Ella? She was never given a choice.

"Okay, dada." Crisis averted. Back to the movie. "Milk please?"

"One piping hot cup of milk, coming right up!" The 27-year-old family patriarch bounded to his feet as the little girl laughed at her father's goofiness. Hot milk, whoever heard of such a thing? Tanner relished these tender moments with his small, yet growing family. Growing because, on this day, the family of three was still a couple weeks away from learning they would be a family of four. Another little person, in nine months' time, to welcome into the baseball life.

"One more loop?" Abigail Peterson, a portrait of grace in running shoes, ran backwards across an unofficial finish line while her husband lumbered to a stop a few steps behind. One would be forgiven for mistaking her for an Olympian and she certainly looked the part while running laps around her husband on a neighborhood track – his deliberate, plodding footfalls kept him well behind his athletic wife. Abigail was in her element in running shoes and, on this occasion (and unnoticed by her husband), she had dusted off her old racing flats just to see how fast she could still fly. A decorated track star at Tulane while her husband-to-be made headlines on the baseball field, it was always a thrill to see if she still had it. She did.

"If you want to carry me home, sure." Bennett Peterson doubled over and rested his hands on his knees. If his wife was an elite, finely tuned running machine, the burly pitcher was quite the opposite. "I'm cooked, baby. Let's call it and go get something to eat."

"Fair enough. You did well today! Are you feeling better?" Abigail rubbed her husband's shoulder while he caught his breath. All of this – the mid-winter running, the assault on his big frame – came with a larger purpose in mind.

"I'm feeling lighter – like a gazelle." He joked, but the truth of the matter was that he *did* feel better. At six-foot-eight and tipping the scale at almost 300 pounds, Peterson wanted to use the offseason to improve his physique. Fresh off a career-year and a multi-year, multi-million dollar contract, he was committed to torturing himself during the winter months so that he could deliver on the promise he made to the Phillies when he signed an extension. He didn't want to be a flash in the pan. He wanted to follow up his breakout campaign by giving the Phillies the three best years of his life. "In all seriousness, it's hard for me, but the results are obvious."

"You know I always think you look good, but you look *good*, you big, handsome, panda bear." Abigail wrapped her arms around her husband and pulled him in for a kiss. It was December and he had already dropped 15 pounds thanks to her coaching. And it wasn't just lip service either – the formula was working. Peterson recognized the value of hard work and knew better than to rest on his laurels after a taste of success. He had made that mistake before and it never worked out particularly well. A 31-year-old reliever with one full season and a half-dozen disappointments under his belt needs to keep fighting, to keep improving. He loved spending time with his family during the offseason, though some part of him couldn't wait to get back to the Phillies' Spring Training home in Clearwater, Florida, to show his coaches and teammates how far he had come. *One step at a time*, he thought. *Still a long way to go.* For the next eight weeks, he would chase his wife around the track and his daughter, Julie, around the house. He would be dad and husband and workout warrior. If he allowed his mind to wander to his most creative delusions, he imagined he was a track star like his wife, hurtling around the rubber track to imagined cheers from an imagined grandstand packed with screaming fans imploring him to run faster and faster still. This was the first offseason he allowed himself to dream of the possibilities, to entertain frivolous thoughts and put his worries behind him. No contract to fight for, no last-minute non-roster invitation to settle on. For the first time in a long and winding career, Peterson had security. And nestled between snowbanks, an icy wind at his back on an empty high school track, he was hell bent on never letting go.

———

The best way to avoid the sophomore slump, that dreaded regression so many rookies endure during their second seasons, is to keep working. To keep running the marathon long after everyone has told you it's okay to stop. For some, like rookie sensation Jose Alvarez, that's just fine.

During his first offseason as a Major Leaguer, Alvarez was not content to bask in the afterglow of a rookie campaign that netted him National League Rookie of the Year honors and heightened expectations about his forthcoming sophomore season. Not long after the Phillies' season ended, Alvarez requested permission from the front office to participate in the Venezuelan Winter League. When that was over, he enrolled in winter courses designed to improve his growing English vocabulary. Alvarez loved his life in America; he wanted to do everything in his power to bridge the gap with his English-speaking teammates. If that meant putting in hard work when he'd be forgiven for hibernating or fleeing to warmer climates, so be it.

"Qué bola, hermano?" *What's up, brother?* The voice on the other end of the line belonged to Alvarez' oldest brother, Javier. Javier, eight years older, was a decorated ballplayer in his own right. After a decade in the Baseball Federation of Cuba, he had played well enough to make a life in baseball, like most men in his family. A jack of all trades, the older Alvarez lacked the elite ability required to catch the eye of visiting U.S. scouts. His dream of playing professional ball began and ended in Cuba and, after more than a decade in the game, he was content with the choices he had made in life and with the baseball career he was grateful to have had in his home country. Javier remained satisfied with his own journey, and excited about his younger brother's success.

"Estoy pinchando, Javier. Siempre." *I'm working, Javier. Always.* The younger Alvarez didn't know any other way to approach his craft. The baseball world had fallen in love with his talent and the potential for how far it could take him in the years to come. Hard work was the only way forward, the only way he knew, and Alvarez just wanted to keep getting better.

"Siempre. Bueno." *Always. Good.* When Javier's playing days were over, there would surely be a place for him in the game. A smart baseball man, he exhibited traits many believed would make him a good manager somewhere down the road – even at the relatively young age of 32. "Es la sola manera." *It is the only way.*

"Sí, sí."

The brothers talked for an hour, maybe longer. Jose and Javier spoke often, even if the elder Alvarez's visits to the U.S. were infrequent. He made it to Philadelphia just in time to watch his baby brother punch a ticket to the postseason on the season's final day. It was his first trip to America, and it came just before the start of his own baseball season, one he was now about a quarter of the way to completing. One thing remained as true today as it was several years earlier when a 16-year-old Jose Alvarez took his first swings in the Cuban National Series, the island nation's largest competitive league: Javier was his brother's biggest fan.

The call ended when Alvarez' teammate, Preston Saunders, arrived at the door. It was mid-December, but the hard work never ended for either man. Saunders, the beating heart of the Phillies' offense atop its young and talented lineup, had found in Alvarez a kindred spirit. Another ballplayer with otherworldly skills and a healthy fear that if he let up, even for just a moment, it might all slip away. And so together, they wouldn't let up. A bond had formed, the language barrier lessening by the day. And if anyone asked what they were up to, toiling away in the dead of winter at the gym or in the batting cage, the answer was always the same for both men: Estoy pinchando.

I'm working.

34

Postscript to a Championship

Baseball is cyclical. Players come, and players go. Players thrive and others fade away. Most of all, the cycle never ends. It just continues, infinitely, with new victors rising to the fore each season and new bottom-dwellers vowing to turn their luck around.

The upstart Phillies team that captured the imagination of an entire region during an improbable playoff run didn't follow up that performance with a World Championship. At least, not right away. At the end of the next season, the Phillies slipped behind the pack and missed the postseason. They would return to the League Championship Series the following year, completing perhaps the most dominant regular season in team history, before once again falling short. In all, it took four seasons before the team stood alone in celebratory euphoria at season's end. Since the team's previous title reign, nearly twenty years slipped by in the blink of an eye for some, a lifetime for others. The latter perspective was held mostly by the Phillies faithful that dotted the stands year after year, through the highest highs and lowest lows. And if you asked the diehards who endured the bad times with hopes that their loyalty would be rewarded, the wait was well worth it.

Aaron Tanner sat in an empty clubhouse, quiet except for highlights from a football game playing in the background. The aroma of champagne was still soaked into the carpet beneath his feet and conjured happy memories for the talented pitcher. Several of the locker stalls surrounding him stood bare, though an occasional jersey or workout shirt still hung alone collecting dust for the winter. Teammates who made their home elsewhere had long cleared out their personal belongings and escaped for the offseason with their laundry and fond memories in tow. Tanner, three weeks removed from his first World Series title, sat drenched in sweat from another hard workout and stared at a photograph resting on a shelf above the rows of jerseys and dress shirts he couldn't quite bring himself to remove after a season he wasn't ready to leave in the past. The photograph featured several men he knew well and one he didn't. Tanner stood arm in arm with his manager, general manager, and Major League Baseball's Commissioner – all smiles, all in their finest formalwear. His team's championship took precedence over any individual accomplishments, but the silver and black Cy Young Award plaque resting in the foreground of the glossy image – recognition of his status as the National League's top pitcher – still counted for something. A box to check, right alongside "World Champion," in what he hoped would be a career people in Philadelphia might talk about long after he had thrown his final pitch.

"How often do you polish that thing at home?" The voice that came from behind him belonged to Mike Brashear and it caused Tanner to turn away from his brief visit with the second-most memorable night of the season. "If I had hardware like that, I don't think I'd ever let it out of my sight."

"Don't you worry, Brash. It's coming." Tanner gave his younger teammate a fist bump and continued to dress.

Brashear, now four seasons into his big league career, also struggled to stay away from the ballpark during the offseason. He liked the feel of it, the smell of the stale corridors that led from the clubhouse to the team's underground batting cages. And, like Tanner, Brashear had developed a reputation as someone who refused to stay away, always getting one more swing in before calling it a day. Always getting a few more reps in before they shut off the lights. He loved the grind – from the beginning, Brashear was more comfortable in a dirt-stained jersey than the designer tuxedos in Tanner's Cy Young Award presentation photograph. "I have a feeling you'll have a few trophies on your mantel by the time your through."

Tanner's prediction was as safe a bet as any. Brashear entered the league with the high expectations that come with being a team's top prospect and after four full seasons, his rocket ship had taken flight. In fact, along with the shrewd signing of Jose Alvarez and the long-term commitment to Preston Saunders, Brashear's emergence was counted by many among the crowning achievements that led the baseball world to honor Phillies GM Mark Johnson as its Executive of the Year in consecutive seasons. And together, the three prime time players and their ace, Aaron Tanner, gave their team a core of talent up the middle of the field that few could match. So, when Tanner predicted accolades for Brashear, it could be argued that he was stating the obvious.

"I just want the big one at the end, that's all." Brashear smiled as he recalled the night when he hoisted the Commissioner's Trophy above his head for the first time. He'd never forget the confetti raining down from the sky or the roar of 45,000 fans experiencing a euphoric bliss seldom replicated in everyday life. For Mike Brashear, one World Championship would never be enough. "Give me that experience at the end of every season and I'll die a happy man."

"That'd be nice, my man. Can't argue with that." The two men shook hands and went their separate ways. Tanner's visits to the ballpark would grow more infrequent as the holidays approached, but as ever, he stayed vigilant in his routine. Amid the pomp and circumstance that comes with a World Series victory and a Cy Young Award, he turned down more publicity and endorsement opportunities than he accepted, remaining focused on balancing his life and his job. It wasn't always easy. Still, he tried to avoid the traps so many others had fallen into before him, the athletes who gave in to the draw of celebrity. No, that lifestyle didn't suit Aaron Tanner and he wasn't about to pretend that it did. Instead, he'd spend the winter focusing on his craft and his family, and then hope that he'd have the chance to do it all over again come April.

John McGown shifted in his seat, tucked in the back of a half-empty sports bar. It was a Monday afternoon and while highlights from Sunday's football games replayed across dozens of big-screen televisions throughout the bar, few patrons milled about at this early hour and even fewer paid any attention to the two men seated at the back of the bar. As afternoon turned to evening, the room would fill with Eagles fans and before long, the sounds of hoots and hollers and the refrain of the fan anthem, "Fly Eagles Fly," would drown out any idle chitchat that might distract from Monday Night Football. And so it was, on a quiet afternoon during his offseason, that McGown sat with *Philadelphia Inquirer* beat writer Tom Flanagan in the middle of football season to talk baseball over a couple of beers.

"Helluva season, John." Tom sat with crossed legs, recorder and notebook in hand.

"That it was. Helluva season."

"Has this offseason been different for you so far? Any changes to your routine now that the Phillies are the talk of the town?" This interview, granted just after the Phillies third World Series title in team history (following 1980 and 2008, respectively) was weeks in the making and the veteran writer was intent on giving the Phillies' under-appreciated field general a proper showcase.

"Nope."

McGown took another sip of his drink and scanned the room. Framed jerseys of Philadelphia sports greats and other memorabilia covered one wall while photos and pennants dotted another. Depending on which teams were in season, the hue of the bar shifted from orange and green during the hockey and football seasons to red every spring and summer. Deep into another offseason, the World Championship frenzy caused a fair amount of red to withstand the encroaching colors and memorabilia of the Flyers, Sixers, and Eagles. Philadelphia was a baseball town again.

"No big-time endorsement deals pouring in for the old man?" Flanagan and McGown shared a laugh at the thought. "I keep waiting to see you on the Tonight Show."

"You'll be waiting for quite some time," McGown replied. "It's not my style."

"I had a good laugh at the guys a couple weeks back on Saturday Night Live. They put on quite a show." The appearance Flanagan referenced was an annual tradition for the big league champs. In the weeks that followed the World Series, a handful of players from the winning team made an appearance every year on the long-running sketch comedy show. "I thought Preston had some good comedic timing."

"He keeps it light in the clubhouse. He doesn't get enough credit for that." McGown couldn't help himself but to bring the conversation back to the clubhouse with praise for his players. It was his way, his custom. Any frivolities that didn't revolve around the diamond made him a little uncomfortable. "Preston Saunders brings a little bit of everything to this team. A lot of everything, to be perfectly honest."

"You really advocate for your guys – that much has been obvious for a decade. I can't help but think it's partly why this team has had so much success in recent years." An observant fan approached and politely interrupted the interview to capture a quick photograph, shake McGown's hand, and express his gratitude. Though he may be more comfortable out of the spotlight, McGown walked on water in Philadelphia.

"The players play the game." McGown's statement was a common refrain in postgame press conferences. Flanagan knew the man well enough to assume that he might hear a few of McGown's favorite attention-deflecting responses during their afternoon together. Through the lean years and during the team's recent success, McGown stayed true to himself. He was, if nothing else, a steadying presence. Always humble, always diverting praise to his ballplayers. "I just draw up the lineup card and try to stay out of their way."

"You don't give yourself enough credit, John." Flanagan jotted down a few notes in his notebook – observations, mostly. Mannerisms and reactions. At the risk of making the old man uncomfortable, Flanagan felt an obligation to offer a little praise to the man who did his best to avoid it.

"I don't need to."

"Fair enough," Flanagan replied, keen on moving to the next topic. "Any concerns heading into a new season?

This is the first time since 2009 that the team will play on Opening Day as defending champs."

"Complacency." McGown didn't hesitate. Complacency was the killer of would-be dynasties. "The baseball season is long. It wears on you. Now that my guys are being fitted for rings, my only concern is that when the road gets hard, they might take their foot off the gas pedal. That's no way to defend a title, and more battle-tested teams than ours have fallen short the next year for just that reason."

"Want an outsider's opinion?"

"Go right ahead," McGown replied, curious to hear the perspective of a man who had covered the ins and outs of the ball club for a decade and a half. It mattered little to McGown that Flanagan didn't spend a great deal of time in the clubhouse or know the players as well as himself. The longtime writer had seen enough baseball through the years to form an educated point of view on the character and composition of the team's most important puzzle pieces.

"Guys like Tanner, Saunders... even Brashear... I don't think one is enough for any of them. In interviews, do you know what they talk about above all else? Do you know what they value most?"

"What's that?"

"The legacy they leave behind here in Philadelphia." At one time or another during his past few years on the beat, Flanagan had heard the word "legacy" spoken from the mouths of the team's cornerstone athletes. It wasn't just talk, either. The team's World Championship was the culmination of years of preparation, though the Phillies' brightest stars only worked harder once the confetti was swept from the city streets. "Have you noticed how often Tanner is in the clubhouse? Brashear? It's almost Christmas, for goodness sakes. They're hungry. I don't think complacency is going to be your problem."

"What then?" McGown folded his arms and leaned across the table, drawing himself closer to his companion.

"You said it yourself – it's a long season. The wear and tear of the grind is your adversary, aside from the Mets, Nationals, and everyone else champing at the bit to take you down."

"I do worry that some of these guys, the core that the rest of this ball club revolves around, push themselves too hard," McGown said. "But it's in their DNA. It's what makes them great at what they do. I won't discourage them from being who they are."

"And that's what makes you great, John. That's why they play so hard for you." Flanagan raised a glass toward McGown, while the manager shook his head and laughed.

"You're relentless, do you know that?"

"I do," Flanagan replied with a wry grin. "It's what makes me great."

"Touché."

Flanagan switched off his recorder and flipped his notebook closed. The first interview, one of several encounters they would have before the first days of the next season, was in the books. The bar stirred to life as the Monday Night Football pregame show began and a couple dozen Eagles fans sidled up to the bar for their first round of drinks. An occasional burst of laughter rose above the din of conversation and two baseball men made their way to the door before either let the draw of a fanatical crowd keep them from home for too much longer. It wasn't quite the same as a late-October ballgame, but something about that sound always drew them back in again. Not today, though. After months on the road, Flanagan and McGown cherished the quiet nights at home.

"Merry Christmas, John. Thanks for giving me some of your time today," Flanagan said with a sturdy handshake. "I'd imagine we can pick this back up in the new year unless something dramatic happens beforehand. I trust you'll text me if anything comes up."

"That I will, Tom. You can count on it. Until then, be well."

They parted, and in the end, almost did make it until the new year before speaking again. On New Year's Eve, true to his word, McGown texted Flanagan with news that the team would announce a new signing when the calendar turned to January. It was a young outfielder by the name of Desi Rodriguez, plucked from Cuba like Jose Alvarez before him. The signing came with measured risk, like any international signing that required a multi-million dollar commitment and came with no guarantee that performance in one nation's baseball circuit would translate on the grandest stage of them all. Of course, it worked out well for the Phillies last time: five seasons after his debut as a highly regarded lottery ticket, Alvarez was everything the team hoped he would become.

And so it goes. Each season brings new players to the big league roster and sends others on to the next chapters of their careers. Some, like Rodriguez, and Alvarez before him, arrive to fanfare. Other players fly under the radar – overlooked until their performance demands attention and they can be overlooked no longer. Successes and failures, heartache and glory, all woven together in the fabric of our National Pastime. From city to city, beneath the bright lights of Philadelphia or on the long bus rides across Small Town America, every game is different and yet, in some ways very much the same. It's a job, and it's a passion. It wears you down and builds you up. It's baseball, and it's beautiful.

Acknowledgments

You've made it to the end of the book! If you've read this story cover to cover, let me start these acknowledgements with a quick "thank you" to you. I hope you, my dear reader, enjoyed this story as much as I enjoyed writing it. And truly, it was a joy to write – I owe that in large part to the many people who so graciously contributed their stories, insights, and perspectives about the game of baseball along the way. *Big League Life* would not have been possible if not for several people who are, quite literally, living the big league life.

The events of *Big League Life* did not happen. This is a work of fiction; the people are figments of my imagination and their stories flowed from some well of creativity in the part of my brain shaped like a baseball diamond. That said, my aim with this novel was to create a world so authentic – so genuine and realistic – that you could almost imagine that the events in this book *did* happen, that the people are real and they are indeed living the big league life. To create this world without input from many others would have been impossible. So, it's with that in mind that I offer my sincerest thanks to:

Ken Korach, the voice of the Oakland Athletics and the voice of summer in the San Francisco Bay Area. I'm grateful for our many email exchanges and phone calls through the years as I fine-tuned the realism of the in-game action and the life of a Major League broadcaster.

To Bill Schlough, an innovative genius who has played a leading role in making the San Francisco Giants one of baseball's most tech-forward franchises, thank you for sharing your perspective on the interactions between ballplayers.

Josh Pahigian, an immensely talented writer and the author of several excellent baseball books, took his editor's pen to an early manuscript and made the final product immeasurably better. Thank you, Josh.

I feel as though this is starting to become a roll call of talented authors, but be that as it may, Scott Butler, blogger and author, deserves high praise for sharing his perspective on an early version of this novel.

"Baseball players don't call their coach 'coach.'" Sage advice from Shane Loux as I tried to boost the authenticity of player/manager interactions.

I'm thankful to Wyatt Mills and Pat Krall for sharing with me their experience of life working their way up the minor league systems of their respective ballclubs.

Thank you to Kaycee Sogard for offering me a glimpse into the life of a ballplayer's wife.

What can I say about Susan Slusser? The longtime baseball writer and former vice president of the Baseball Writer's Association gave me a behind-the-scenes look at the life of a beat writer. From the press box to the clubhouse, from the long road trips to the late nights.

One of my favorite conversations during this entire journey was a lengthy phone call with former ballplayer and pro scout, Chris Knabenshue. His contribution to making this novel a reading experience that rings true and hits an authentic note cannot be overstated. So grateful for you, Chris.

To my publisher, Sherri, thanks for believing in me from the very beginning. You made my first book *Diehards* a reality and took on this new challenge with such enthusiasm. I am, truly, a "diehard" of Rowe Publishing!

My wife deserves more praise than I could possibly offer in this section. She's been an early reader, a sounding board, an editor, a problem-solver, a psychiatrist, and so much more. Thank you for your love and support all these years, Leah.

Nick and Coop, I know it's not the A's, but I hope you find yourself rooting for this fictional version of the Fightin' Phils by the end of the story. A shared passion for this great game, spanning many years and even more ballgames, solidified our friendship and I'm thankful to you both for the many hours we've spent talking baseball.

Eric, hope this story adds to your enjoyment of the game we love.

Beth, Jeff, and Jane, I'm always grateful for your enthusiasm and interest in my writing projects. Hope you enjoy this one.

Liv and May, I cherish our time together watching ballgames and I always will. I look forward to sharing this story with you as you grow older; I hope, in time, it adds new layers to your understanding and enjoyment of pro ball.

To RW, an observer of my Philadelphia Phillies fandom who, while not a sports fan himself, raised me in a manner that allowed my own sports obsession to grow. Thanks for all your support and encouragement all these years.

Mom, this one's for you.

About the Author

Chip Scarinzi is an award-winning communications executive by trade and a dyed-in-the-wool baseball fan at heart. A lifelong Philadelphia sports fan, he lives with his wife and two young daughters in the shadow of the Oakland Coliseum in nearby Alameda, Calif.

Scarinzi's first book, *Diehards: Why Fans Care So Much About Sports*, was the manifestation of his own passion for sports and a desire to understand why he and his tribe care so much about games.

While a work of fiction, *Big League Life* is the result of years of research interviews, and first-hand accounts provided by several men and women who call the "big league life" their life.

———

Author can be directly contacted through:

Website: www.chipscarinzi.com

Twitter: @ScarinziSports

Facebook: www.facebook.com/ChipScarinziBooks

Other Books by the Author

Diehard sports fans are
arguably the beating heart of the
sports industry. In good times and
in bad, they file into stadiums and
arenas of all shapes and sizes ready
to expend financial and emotional
currency on a hobby that goes
horribly wrong half of the time.

Why do diehards invest so fully
in sports teams and players when
that commitment, love and adoration is
seldom reciprocated – if ever?

Through the lens of baseball, *Diehards: Why Fans
Care So Much About Sports* unravels the mystery of
sports fans and provides context for what fuels the
evolution from casual fan to diehard. In *Diehards*, Chip
Scarinzi canvasses experts about the impact of sports
fandom on fan psyche, health, and family life while also
sharing personal accounts of deep-seated sports passion
from the most dedicated of fans.

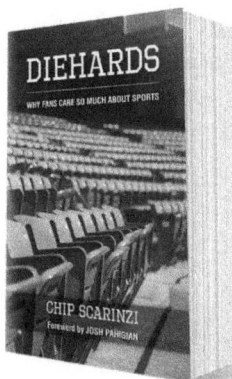

———

"For the true fan of baseball, reading Diehards *is like sitting in your season seats and trading stories of euphoria and
defeat with the other fanatic regulars around you."* —**Heidi
Watney**, MLB Network

"Through this fine book – that is as lively and humorous as it is well researched and insightful – [Scarinzi] has brought me to a deeper understanding of my own obsession." —**Josh Pahigian**, author of *The Ultimate Baseball Road Trip* and *101 Baseball Places to See Before You Strike Out*

"... the heart and soul of Diehards *is the cast of characters Chip meets along the way: Superfan Will MacNeil, 'Banjo Man,' Father Jim Greanias, along with the long forgotten St. Louis Browns and 'Baseball Heaven' in St. Louis."* — **Scott Butler,** Editor of *Phils Baseball* for the Philadelphia Phillies